FROM DESPAIR TO HOPE

Farid Daya

FROM DESPAIR TO HOPE

Journeys across conflict, post-conflict and disaster zones, immersed in faith & service

By
Farid Daya

As narrated to Aditi Khanna

© Copyright 2025 by Farid Daya. All rights reserved.

It is not legal to reproduce, duplicate or transmit any part of this document in either electronic means or printed format. Recording of this publication is strictly prohibited.

Dedication

This book is dedicated to:

- His Highness the Aga Khan and the Ismaili Council for tireless community initiatives in the UK;
- FOCUS Humanitarian Assistance;
- and the Aga Khan Development Network's (AKDN) humanitarian, development and peacebuilding missions around the world.

This is a tribute to the life and legacy of His Highness Aga Khan IV, Prince Karim Al-Husseini, who passed away on February 4, 2025, in Lisbon, Portugal. All references to His Highness in the following chapters relate to Aga Khan IV.

Acknowledgments

When I set out on this journey to document the many ups and downs, twists and turns of a fulfilling career in humanitarian work, it was with much anticipation and some trepidation. The approximately 16-month journey of penning down these thoughts and experiences has been made possible only with the support of my loving family, D'jemilla, Rasool, Nabila and Rahim and siblings Shahnaz, Mehboob and Naznin, to whom I want to express my fondest gratitude.

However, this appreciation is by no means restricted to just the documenting process but also to the many years of upheavals and worries that they would have undoubtedly endured while I was away on one of the many missions I have recounted in the preceding pages. I thank them profusely for their unwavering support, encouragement and understanding.

Throughout these chapters of my life's journey, which I consider blessed by God's grace, the one hand that has guided me through every step of the way is the inspiration and profound commitment of His Highness to alleviating the suffering of humanity and his commitment to support those most in need. It is this guiding light that shines for each and every one of us fortunate to be able to lend a helping hand, in our own small ways.

Here, I would like to pay tribute to the leaders of the institutions, namely the Ismaili Councils, Focus Humanitarian Assistance and Aga Khan Foundation, for their confidence in me and hundreds of staff, volunteers and international aid workers who I have had the good fortune to work alongside over the years. Their selfless dedication to the cause in some of the most extenuating circumstances has certainly influenced the title of this book – fighting the despair to bring a ray of hope to millions.

Last, but by no means the least, my sincere gratefulness to Karim Mawji, for throwing his wholehearted support behind this project; and to Anar Nanji for the editor's touch and Minaz Nanji for designing the beautiful cover and selecting the appropriate images for this effort to shine a light on the Ismaili community's many uncharted endeavours to make the world a happier and peaceful place for one and all.

About the Author

Farid Daya has dedicated his life to humanitarian action, development and peacebuilding efforts around the world. He has an inspiring track record of delivering complex programmes in conflict and post-conflict zones and coordinating rebuilding projects in the aftermath of natural disasters under challenging circumstances, blending academic rigour with extensive field experience.

With a master's degree in development management, bolstered by tailored courses in humanitarian operations, project management, diplomacy, conflict resolution and resource mobilisation, Farid honed his skills in combining strategic thinking with hands-on implementation.

From Despair to Hope is Farid's first book, structured as a memoir to capture his engaging style and affable nature, which helped him create strong stakeholder support and buy-in of partners, donors and international agencies during his many humanitarian missions worldwide. It is designed to take the reader on a journey from Africa to Europe, via Central Asia, the Middle East and Indian Subcontinent, traversing mountains, rivers, snow and sand across cities and remote villages by land, water and air. The narrative, backed up by vivid images and a light touch approach to some quite stark experiences, will hopefully make readers not only feel a part of his incredible life journey but also motivated to set out on a similar path of hope.

Farid is now based in London with his wife D'jemilla, who along with their children Rasool, Nabila and Rahim have been resolute supporters of his passion for adventure and willingness to tackle risks head on, dating right back to his days as a Boy Scout.

Contents

Foreword 1
Introduction 9
Chapter One Afghanistan – Humanity Overcoming Upheavals............ 21
    Flight into the Unknown.. 23
    Finding My Feet 26
    Coffee Diplomacy 29
    On Our Way… 33
    Internal Fissures 35
    Ground Assessments 36
    Frugal Engineering.. 39
    Home Turf 42
    Back in Time 43
    Review and Analysis 46
    Crossing Points 50
    Horse Ride to Remember 52
    Hand of God 54
    The Great Game 56
    Food for Work 58
    Bridge to the Future... 61
    Post-Taliban Landscape 63
    Close Shave with Death... 65
    Buddhas of Bamiyan 67
    Looking to the Future 70
    Earthquake Relief.. 74
Chapter Two Syria – Resilience In An Active War Zone 99

    Shift of Focus 100
    Deathly Fireworks 102
    Life Must Carry On 105
    Lasting Impact 109
    Long-Term View 112
Chapter Three Russia – An Expedition Breaking New Ground 135
    Stark Contrasts 137
    Getting Started 139
    Finding Our Feet 141
    Working Within Parameters 144
    Life as Expatriates 151
Chapter Four Interventions of Compassion 161
    MOZAMBIQUE – Cyclone Leon-Eline (2000) 161
    INDIA – Earthquake in Bhuj, Gujarat (2001) 176
    Boxing Day Tsunami (2004) 196
    Kashmir Earthquake (2005) 205
    MADAGASCAR – Cyclone Gafilo (2004) 218
Conclusion 230
Epilogue 234
About AKDN 236
    Founder and Chairman 236
    FOCUS Humanitarian Assistance 238

Foreword

I have known Farid since 1985 when he took up his post as Admin Officer at the newly opened Ismaili Centre in South Kensington, London, a couple of years after the Silver Jubilee celebrations by the global Ismaili Muslim Jamat, marking the 25 years of His Highness the Aga Khan's Imamat. It was at a time when the Ismaili Muslim community was establishing its roots, expanding and strengthening its institutional base for community governance and to serve the wider society, in the UK and internationally.

Farid arrived to take up his post at the Ismaili Centre at a time when the community demanded from everyone their maximum attention and contribution in terms of professional and voluntary service to meet the needs of resettlement, governance and development. At that time, I was serving as the Chairman of the Aga Khan Foundation (AKF) UK's National Committee, and experienced first-hand what it was like to be part of this foundation-laying phase of the Ismaili community in the UK.

I was aware that since 1985, Farid had served in the Ismail Community and the AKDN institutions and had worked in several countries in Asia, Africa and Europe in the field of governance, development and humanitarian assistance. So, when Farid told me that he had written a memoir of his career as a source of inspiration to the younger members of the Jamat and complimented me by inviting me to write a Foreword, I immediately agreed as a matter of honour.

It was not until I actually read the memoirs that I realised that what Farid had done was to document an incredible account of his life journey of service to the Ismaili community and to the society at large, in the UK and overseas. Farid was brought up by his family to be a man of faith in the Ismaili Muslim tradition and a true *murid* (disciple) of the Imam of the time. It seems that Farid's fate was sealed when his name Farid, the unique one, was bestowed upon him at birth by Imam Sultan Mohamed Shah, the grandfather of His Highness the Aga Khan Shah Karim Al Hussaini Hazar Imam. Farid himself wonders, as documented in his memoir, whether it was this prescient naming that was to shape his destiny.

The memoir, as told to London-based journalist and writer Aditi Khanna, is a moving record of an extraordinary career spent in development and humanitarian assistance, serving the needs of communities in conflict and disaster zones; often without knowing what challenges, surprises, unknowns and successes or failures lay in store. It records Farid's "many experiences and encounters, stories of loss and suffering but above all hope – hope that the human spirit can triumph over the most impossible odds.

Such a career is not for everyone but reserved for only a few like Farid, who from his very early days carried that special light of faith in his heart and compelling urge to serve his Imam, his community and the wider society. This was poignantly captured by an insightful counsellor during a career counselling session at the time when Farid was studying for an MBA degree while working at the Ismaili Centre. He was advised that an MBA was not for him because he was focused on helping people as his bottom line and not making money, and that he should consider a career in development.

As Farid notes: "That was my moment of epiphany. I had found my purpose!" And, this was immediately followed by his reflection that "life has a way of bringing us face to face with our destiny and mine was with the AKDN". Thus began Farid's career in development and humanitarian assistance in 1995, comprising of a set of assignments most often into the unknown over several decades. According to him, the touchstones which capture Farid's true working spirit well were: "whatever it takes, aid must be given into the hands of the beneficiaries in a manner that preserves their dignity" and "whoever saves a life it is as though he had saved the lives of all mankind *(Quran 5:32)*."

Arriving at his "dream come true" moment to become involved in AKDN's field work took Farid some two decades of spiritual and heartfelt yearning while working with the Ismaili Council in Kenya and in the UK. It was, therefore, to be expected when he was appointed in January 2000 to the role of Programme Manager, Programme – Afghanistan, at FOCUS Europe when his "journey into conflict and disaster zones began in all earnest", where he found himself in the deep end with a firm resolve to "make a difference in whatever little way that I can".

Farid is a self-effacing, kind and quiet man with an unmistakable presence, exhibiting much humility, gratitude and limitless patience. It would therefore not be in keeping with his character to make a drumbeating display of the unusual and often life-threatening and risky work he was engaged in much of the time. Indeed, Farid thus became an integral part of the global AKDN development and humanitarian assistance organisation engaged in serving communities, locally and internationally.

Farid was always ready to serve anywhere and, in any situation, and indeed that is what he ended up doing during his career. His memoirs provide gripping and unimaginable accounts of his involvement in the development and humanitarian assistance initiatives in Afghanistan, Syria and Russia as well as of his involvement, without any advance warning, in the emergency disaster response missions or interventions to Mozambique, India, Kashmir and Madagascar.

At the time Afghanistan was in a state of upheaval under the rule of the Taliban and needed both emergency aid and development support; Syria was an active war zone and in need of support to remain resilient, including against ISIS; and Russia was emerging from its earlier clock of Communism that required breaking new grounds. Each assignment of several years in Afghanistan, Syria and Russia and each emergency missions to disaster zones created by the cyclone in the north and north-east of Mozambique, or by the earthquake at Bhuj in Gujarat, India and the tsunami along the eastern coastline and regions in India, or earthquake in Kashmir, Pakistan, or the cyclone in the eastern and north-easter Madagascar, presented a different set of challenges and risks, often life threatening and to be tackled with dedication, resolve and sheer grit, which only a few people like Farid are fortunate enough to possess.

It would not be an exaggeration to say that much of the humanitarian assistance work which Farid undertook would easily be considered to be of the "mission impossible" nature but in every case, Farid was able to conclude that the interventions he was part of always led to bringing hope in situations where there was despair and despondency. To Farid, these were interventions of compassion, delivering emergency aid directly to the families caught up and suffering from the disasters. This memoir takes the reader behind the scenes where one can observe at close hand what it takes to ignite the spark of hope for people who are in a state of despair. At the same time, Farid also provides, with some humour, a glimpse of some real-life situations at the everyday level of human existence which he experienced on the ground and in the air, reminding us that even at the time of disasters, normal life activities continue with ingenuity to meet economic and cultural human needs.

This memoir does total justice to the title of the book: 'From Despair to Hope: Journeys across conflict, post-conflict and disaster zones, immersed in faith & service'. As Farid points out: "In my humble view, there can be no greater calling in life than to strive towards that hope which shines through the depths of despair". Indeed, it is almost impossible for any human being to engage seriously year after year in such journeys into the unknown without a strong spiritual foundation in one's faith in the Almighty, which in Islam exhorts the faithful to serve mankind which has been created from a single soul.

Aditi Khanna in the Epilogue sums up succinctly in the following words what his memoir relays. "The pre-eminent emotion that best defines Farid's retelling of assignments is a profound sense of duty, shared in equal measure by D'jemilla (Farid's wife). Asked how she coped with her husband's radio silences knowing he was somewhere deep into a warzone, especially during the days pre-dating mobile phone connectivity, D'jemilla responded with the same equanimity as her husband – 'I knew he was doing his duty'." In actual fact, she too was doing her duty in enabling Farid to undertake the superhuman assignments, even accompanying him on occasion.

In the Muslim tradition, the word 'Duty' – or *faraj* in Gujarati or *fard* in Arabic – carries a deeply spiritual and moral connotation, because in Islam, *fard* or *farz* refers to an obligatory action or duty that every Muslim is required to fulfil. It is a religious duty commanded by Allah. *Farz* encompasses a range of responsibilities prescribed by Allah, which serve as a means of spiritual growth, discipline, and submission to His will.

Farid's memoir end with the following final statement by the writer: "I have tried to do complete justice to his incredibly inspiring life journey and hope that it can serve to motivate others to step into the field of humanitarian assistance. In his own words, it is not just a job but a true calling and an extremely satisfying life mission."

It has been a real privilege and an honour for me to contribute this Foreword to this book. In some ways this memoir represents all of us because there is a yearning in every one of us to be virtuous and contribute to the wellbeing of humanity. However, only a few people like Farid are fortunate to have been blessed with the wherewithal and abilities to discharge special duties in the most difficult of circumstances to deliver hope-inducing humanitarian assistance.

This memoir will remain a source of happiness not only to Farid and his family but also to those who have been involved in development and humanitarian assistance work, as well as anyone who reads the book and is inspired by it.

■ Professor Amir Kassam OBE, FRSB, CBiol, PhD is a Visiting Professor in the School of Agriculture, Policy and Development, University of Reading, UK, where he teaches a post-graduate course entitled 'Rethinking Agriculture: Implementing Solutions'. He was awarded an OBE in the Queen's Honours List in 2005 for services to tropical agriculture and to rural development. Prof. Kassam is an adviser in sustainable agriculture intensification with Food and Agriculture Organisation (FAO), Rome, and with The Aga Khan Foundation.

Introduction

> There is no force more powerful or more needed today. When we plant hope in people's lives, we lighten all their burdens. It is a source of energy and inspiration that is endlessly renewable.
>
> His Highness the Aga Khan (March 2023)

Disasters, natural or manmade, shatter hopes that soon turn to despair. Human interventions attempt to turn these situations of despair back to hope.

There is no greater sense of gratification than working towards and then witnessing this transition from despair to hope - some instant but many only a promise of what could be. However, an enduring thread of such meaningful interventions is the countless stories that emerge - stories of courage, grit and determination, fear and sacrifice, and even some of inevitable heartbreak.

But these are stories that resonate across continents and manmade boundaries and help demonstrate that humanity prevails in situations of hopelessness. Over decades of working in conflict and disaster zones, both natural and manmade, I have encountered countless such situations of despair. Looking back, I pushed through the toughest of challenges without much reflection and only now feel it may be time to stop and dwell on some of those stories that have shone through a lifetime of being blessed with the grace and abundance of being given an opportunity to serve.

My work through the humanitarian missions undertaken as part of the Aga Khan Development Network (AKDN) and with Focus Humanitarian Assistance, an affiliate of AKDN, was most definitively my calling. No salary, benefits or incentives could quantify the bounty of such a task. There were indeed some life-or-death scenarios, coming face to face with danger and losing close associates to bombings just yards away, but it is the grace and abundance of one's calling that sees one through such haunting moments.

I was born to a loving family home of humble means in Nairobi, Kenya, in 1956 – not in a hospital but ensconced within a caring community support network of a housing cooperative where my parents, Gulshan and Kassamali, had acquired a home just before my birth. I was named Farid, the unique one, a name bestowed upon me by His Highness the Aga Khan's grandfather at the time – Sir Sultan Mohamed Shah. Was it this prescient naming that was to shape my destiny? I wonder.

Historically, our Khoja strand of the Ismaili Muslim community from the Subcontinent (India, Pakistan, Bangladesh) has its roots in the Kutch region of Gujarat, western India, dating back to the 1800s. The local traditions of devotional recitations were transformed into *ginans* (knowledge) to spread the Ismaili message of the oneness of

God and other tenets of the faith of Islam and of the Shia interpretation under the lineage of a living Imam – a direct descendant of the Prophet Mohamed, *may peace be upon Him and his family*.

The earliest community members to immigrate to East Africa from the Indian Subcontinent first established their foothold in Zanzibar in the 1800s, although community merchants and other traders based in western India had been trading in the western Indian Ocean region since at least the seventeenth century. Traders used the northeast Monsoon winds to travel across the Indian Ocean with their merchandise, often at sea for a month or longer in harsh conditions. When the Monsoon winds changed direction to southwest, the traders would return home with their wares.

The early community settlers in Zanzibar were farmers, who were compelled to emigrate due to successive droughts and famines that had caused economic hardships, further magnified by the British Empire's industrialisation and economic policies. Eventually large numbers of community members of diverse backgrounds began to set out for new lands with the blessings of the 48th Imam His Highness Sultan Mohamed Shah, the grandfather of the current Imam – His Highness Prince Karim Aga Khan. When Zanzibar became the Omani capital in 1832, it provided political stability and security as well as enhanced economic opportunities for traders to expand their businesses.

By the end of the nineteenth century, when the interior of East Africa was becoming more accessible through the construction of roads and railways, an increasing number of trading establishments moved from Zanzibar to the East African mainland, resulting in large numbers of Indians, including many from the Ismaili Muslim community, moving inland. It was at around this time that waves of our community spread across Zanzibar in Tanzania, Mombasa in Kenya, with others settling in Uganda and Rwanda. Madagascar, a French colony, and Mozambique, a Portuguese colony, and South Africa were some of the other hubs. According to my older brother's research, my great, great grandfather Daya and his wife Hirbai arrived in Zanzibar in 1880. My parents were born there and moved to Kenya, a British colony at the time, after their marriage in 1947. My older siblings and I were all born in Kenya, where the English language became our mainstay.

By the time I came into the world, our compact home in Nairobi was a hive of family activity as relatives from all parts of East Africa would often converge upon the capital city for healthcare or other needs only met in a large metropolis. As a result, I recall an idyllic childhood that may not have been plentiful in monetary terms but was boundless in happy memories of family gatherings. The shared communal *verandah* of the cooperative-style tenement leant itself to an extremely convivial setting with the neighbours, be it sharing each other's food, babysitting facilities or other aspects of a warm extended support network.

As the fourth of five children, I can now see how I must have been quite a handful. It would be fair to say that I spent a disproportionate amount of time playing marbles or *gilli danda* (a simplistic Indian game played with a stick and a small piece of wood) with the neighbourhood kids than completing my school homework. Behind our home was a valley leading up to the river, which technically being forbidden territory only served to make it our most favoured playing ground.

My father's work as a butcher and mother's tailoring meant we were at best comfortable but also in need of supplementary income, which involved my mother taking on additional sewing jobs or cooking up *vitumbua* sweet dumplings for deliveries by my older brother on foot. Our cooperative living meant we always had access to transport, telephone and other such amenities with a little help from our friends and neighbours, and soon there was even the luxury of a black and white television set which a cluster of families from the neighbourhood enjoyed together.

As a child, I recall that airplanes always held a fascination for me, never having flown in one. Somehow in my mind's eye these passenger aircraft only ever flew to London – the only place that my childish imagination had conjured up as the faraway land I would one day love to fly out to and come back bearing gifts for everyone in the family. Ironically, when I did set off on my first plane journey, it was indeed for London in 1975, but it would be many years before this city which is now very much home would come to feel as such.

The timing of my birth before Kenya gained independence gave me the option of taking up British citizenship or becoming a Kenyan citizen before I turned 18. My parents and older siblings were already Kenyan citizens and one of my older sisters had settled in Canada. With the crises in neighbouring Uganda still looming in the minds of the families of South Asian descent, the motivations to send one or more family members to another country were high. The timing was right for me to opt for British citizenship, and I viewed the move to London more as another adventure, like my Boy Scout days when we went camping, mountain climbing and the like.

My first flight was booked for London on August 5, 1975. It was on a one-way ticket with no one to meet me at the airport when I landed in the capital of the United Kingdom amidst an uncharacteristic heatwave. Is this really London? Can't be, I thought, because the London from our television sets was meant to be cold, grey and rainy with people snuggled in overcoats. It was only as I drove up from the airport into the city and saw a sign of the energy drink Lucozade atop the then GlaxoSmithKline (GSK) building on the A4 that a sense of familiarity helped overcome the trepidation somewhat - that's a drink we knew well in Kenya and seeing it emblazoned across the skyline offered a strange sense of reassurance. In yet another ironic twist, years later it is that very building - now converted into flats - which would become home to me and my wife.

I met D'jemilla in Nairobi at a time when I had returned homesick after five years of London schooling, which had felt more like an exile. I declared categorically to my mother that I would never be going back to England because I simply missed home too much. Even though D'jemilla and I went to the same school as kids and she lived next door, we never really knew each other. Perhaps one can call it fate, but we were clearly destined for each other by the time we were eventually introduced by her sister at the sports club I frequented.

I won't say the rest is history because in a way it was this union that triggered a series of serendipitous developments in both our lives. It was when I went over to collect our marriage certificate from the local Ismaili Council Office that an informal role helping out with their accounts opened up following an extended visit by His Highness the Aga Khan and couples married around the time had the added fortune of being blessed by him. So, it was His Highness who joined our hands in blessing.

Now, all these years later, we recall that a petition of sorts was being circulated to collate signatures of those in the community who were willing to offer their unconditional services to His Highness and the community. D'jemilla and I look back and ponder: how naïve were we to sign up to such a profound commitment? But perhaps it was that moment of destiny that was to go on to define the rest of our lives. It is no wonder that D'jemilla has her own inspiring stories to tell of service to the community in various countries as a volunteer specialist in Early Childhood Development (ECD).

To this day, she has been a rock of support through all the treacherous, and often petrifying, travels I have undertaken to warzones and disaster-hit countries. She was often questioned why she did not rebel or demand I stay as I set off, even when she was heavily pregnant with one of our three beautiful children. But it was our shared value system and joint commitment to service that has endured over the course of our marriage, even to this day as we took on the role as Head of our community's West London Jamatkhana in July 2023.

In many ways, it is a continuation of a journey which began in all earnest in 1981, when I started as a volunteer for our local council to help out with the accounts while I assisted with my elder brother's accountancy firm. The part-time work at the Ismaili Council gradually took on a much wider scope in 1982 as we prepared for His Highness' Silver Jubilee celebrations in Nairobi.

I relished the additional responsibilities, and the hours were also good because it meant I had quality time on my hands as a newly married man. That was, in many ways, my first taste of community service, handling various aspects of organisational work for the Ismaili Council in Nairobi. But there was a clear lack of long-term career direction until 1985, when a role opened up for an Administrative Officer at the Ismaili Centre which had been newly built in London's South Kensington area. It involved a broad brush of responsibilities, including supporting the centre's facilities and programmes of the Ismaili Council in the UK, which covered a wide range of activities from education and health to economic development and social welfare, encompassing youth projects within the social and sporting spheres.

So, after nearly a decade since my first visit as an anxious and inexperienced student, I was back in London in April 1985 with a young family that now included a three-year-old toddler son. D'jemilla was pregnant with our daughter at the time and the first six months of finding our feet in a new city was not the easiest. However, with the community support network in the Jamatkhana, things soon settled down to a nice rhythm. In many ways, it signifies the cycle of life that today D'jemilla and I are working for our Jamatkhana offering similar support to others who would be starting out on their own life journeys.

Inspired by the present His Highness the Aga Khan's guidance on lifelong learning, I felt it was time to broaden my own academic horizons and took on the challenge of studying for one of the management training MBA modules at the Open University with the support of the Ismaili Council. It involved a summer school based at the campus of a UK university with an option to interact with a Career Counsellor. Until that point in life, I wasn't convinced that a counsellor could offer much insight into the best career path to pursue. I felt I was on the path that was right for me. However, I hesitantly signed up for it and half-way through our one-hour slot the counsellor categorically declared that an MBA is not for me.

To illustrate his point, he referenced two different character types: the first involves people who are focussed on profit as the bottom line and the second is made of those for whom the bottom line is people. He explained: "And you belong in the second category. Have you considered a career in the development sphere?" That was my moment of epiphany. I had found my purpose!

Life has a way of bringing us face to face with our destiny and mine was with the Aga Khan Development Network (AKDN). I was asked by the President of the Ismaili Council for the United Kingdom to join him for the groundwork required for a visit to Russia by His

Highness in January 1995. It was my first-hand experience of AKDN in action, making a real difference to people's lives on the ground. Later that year, His Highness visited Tajikistan and that is when he started to establish institutions there. This was followed up by another visit in 1998. For these visits, I was part of the "advance team" ahead of major visits by His Highness to Central Asia.

Around the time that the Taliban took over Afghanistan in 1998, a Humanitarian Aid Emergency Operating Centre was established at the Ismaili Centre in London – I was deeply embedded in this initiative, by then certain that this was exactly the kind of work that I wanted to dedicate my life to. The pathways opened up, with the President asking me to join the humanitarian arm of the AKDN – Focus Humanitarian Assistance Europe Foundation.

There were three Focus Offices set up – one each in the US, Canada and Europe – with each developing its specific expertise. Focus Canada was working on migration and refugee resettlement and Focus USA was geared towards GPS technology for assistance related to natural disasters such as droughts and floods. Focus Europe was earmarked for manmade and natural disasters, and I was appointed to the role of Programme Manager, Programme – Afghanistan.

This was in January 2000, when my journey into conflict and disaster zones began in all earnest and the following chapters will go on to document the many experiences and encounters, stories of loss and suffering but above all hope - hope that the human spirit can triumph over the most impossible odds.

What follows is an account from that point onwards, with the chapters divided along the lines of the countries and regions that I covered during the course of my humanitarian work around the world. The motto was always: whatever it takes, aid must be given into the hands of the beneficiaries in a manner that preserves their dignity.

> "And whoever saves a life it is as though he had saved the lives of all mankind"
>
> - Quran 5:32

Chapter One
Afghanistan – Humanity Overcoming Upheavals

It was as Programme Manager, Programme Afghanistan, for FOCUS Humanitarian Assistance (Europe) that my humanitarian action and development journey began in earnest. I found myself in the deep end, with a firm resolve to make a difference in whatever little way that I can.

The year was 2000 and by then the Taliban had taken charge of most of the country except the Badakshan region. Our humanitarian activities, however, served a wider region, with Afghan Badakshan being accessed through neighbouring Tajikistan and headquartered at a town named Khorog. The other parts of Afghanistan were served through the Pakistan capital of Islamabad. My brief as the new Programme Manager from London was to have oversight of our humanitarian assistance programme – both from our base in Khorog and Islamabad.

With no presence on the ground in the Taliban-held regions, it was from these neighbouring hubs that the United Nations (UN) and other aid agencies also conducted their humanitarian operations. Our FOCUS mission was to work in harmony with the UN, non-governmental agencies (NGOs) active in the region and donors. I felt more than mentally prepared for this leap into the unknown – having worked on His Highness' visits to Tajikistan in the 1990s. At the time, I recall the extremely stark contrast across the Panj River that served as a border between Tajikistan and Afghanistan – the Tajik side was quite developed with electricity, roads and solid infrastructure but just across the river, all that was visible was at best a donkey track and small villages with mud brick structures dotted along the valley. This memory from that visit, when we organised food distribution facilities across the river, served as my first-hand knowledge of the enormous task ahead in my new role.

I felt eager to be a part of things more proactively and was even excited at the prospect of this new challenge, even though it meant I would no longer be doing this work from the relative comfort of the Tajikistan side of the border but embedded in the very heart of war-torn Taliban territory – unchartered waters to say the least!

The harsh and oppressive landscape of the anti-Shia sentiments that pervaded the Taliban-held regions at the time forced several Afghans, especially those with the means to escape, to flee the region to neighbouring Pakistan. Others were compelled to comply with the demand of the Taliban militia for the conscription of one of their sons, who were then used as human fodder on the frontlines of the war with the West. Many of the struggling families would resort to offering blood money to protect their loved ones and help them escape armed combat. Such were the complexities and challenges of the terrain I would be operating in.

But as I took charge of my new placement with Programme Afghanistan in London on 1 January 2000, I felt ready for a very different kind of combat – the mission to try and make a difference in a land I knew was in desperate need of a helping hand from FOCUS, guided by His Highness' vision for humanitarian support based on the needs and active participation of the local communities.

Flight into the Unknown

The route to Taliban-held Afghanistan was quite a circuitous one – flying from London to Islamabad after obtaining a Pakistan visa where I had to go through the laborious task of acquiring the all-important Taliban visa to enter Afghanistan. However, this visa was of no use when it came to gaining access to the Badakshan region, for which I needed a bespoke "Rabbani Visa" – named after the leader Burhanuddin Rabbani who controlled the Islamic Emirate of Badakshan at the time. Each time I visited, my passport also was stamped with entry and exit visas. I would go on to use several passport booklets over the course of the next 18 years.

For a registered charity like ours operating in the region to assist the locals, acquiring these tricky documents did not prove overly problematic. However, getting access to the region itself was a whole different matter – with no commercial air traffic connectivity to the area or even a fully functional airport in the Afghan capital of Kabul. Therefore, it transpired that the only way for me to land in this unchartered territory was in a UN scheduled plane.

As I walked up to the designated section for UN flights at Islamabad Airport, a demarcated zone away from the airport's regular international air traffic, I found myself face to face with a group of rather sombre-looking co-passengers. Each of us was sizing the other up, somewhat suspiciously, as we wondered about the unknown companions thrown together on this collective journey into the unknown. This was the moment that I recall my first palpable sense of dread – I was embarking into treacherous territory with very little knowledge of what awaited me in the warzone at the other end of this chartered flight.

Is my beard long enough, was a thought that flashed across my mind? Under the Taliban decree at the time, all men were required to sport facial hair of a specified length. While there was an exemption in place for foreigners, I was acutely aware of my disadvantage of being a foreigner who did not particularly "look" foreign due to my South Asian heritage. I had read reports of fierce officials from the Ministry for the Propagation of Virtue and Prevention of Vice punishing men with lashings for minor transgressions, such as shorter than stipulated beards, before they are given a chance to proffer an explanation.

These were the kind of dreadful scenarios playing out in my mind in that small waiting room, which I shared with a motley crew of foreigners and locals, all avoiding eye contact with each other. Of course, I would go on to find things were smoother on the ground than I feared, largely down to our FOCUS Europe marked car and the ground staff ensuring they sported the right length of beards. But that was all to come later; at this moment, it felt like I was preparing for a bungee jump, hoping that the harness would do the desired job on the day!

Nonetheless, as a minibus ferried us over to the tarmac, I felt a sense of privilege to be one among a handful of strangers to have a seat on that UN plane. Our destination was Mazar-e-Sharif, an architectural gem of an Afghan city famous for the shrine of Ali. As soon as we touched down and started our shaky walk towards a nondescript terminal building, that special UN plane had already taken off for its return flight to Islamabad. There was another momentary sense of trepidation as I realised that I was now officially on less-than-friendly terrain, a feeling that heightened by degrees as all my co-passengers were swiftly cleared one by one for exit – either due to their local Afghan passports or by virtue of being UN staffers.

As the only traveler on that charter with a British passport, I spent some very anxious moments that felt much longer than the few hours I had to wait while the gentleman who had taken my passport for scrutiny returned with the requisite stamp. "Be kind to your guests" - the English translation of an Arabic proverb from the 'Quran' stared back at me from a wall in the terminal building. It gave me an inexplicable sense of reassurance about my safe exit as I quietly reflected on the fact that this beautiful proverb having survived the test of time through Afghanistan's many political upheavals hopefully meant they still believed in treating visitors with some kindness.

My thoughts then shifted to what was in store once I did make it out of the rather unusual passport control zone. Will our local support officers be waiting for me, as arranged? What would I do if they weren't there for some reason? What are my next steps? There were multiple questions playing around in my mind as I was in an airport without any of the usual sign-posting that directs travellers out into the city.

Finding My Feet

A wave of relief engulfed me as I spotted our local Afghan officials, Engineer Kudhus and Zabi, on finally emerging from the terminal building clutching at my freshly Taliban-stamped passport.

There they were in a designated Focus Humanitarian Assistance minivan ready to ferry me off to my new assignment. However, there were some hurdles still to come - I may now be officially stamped to be in the country, but its strict curfew laws meant we must be indoors by 1600 local time before the city's intermittent power is completely switched off by 1800. Those were the rules in theory and not particularly keen to find out what a failure to comply with them would mean, we made a dash for it!

It was many weeks before I eventually became accustomed to some of these stringent laws of the land, which also forbade any music or cinematic distractions on our devices. We were never quite sure who among the locals might report perceived transgressors to the Ministry of Vice and Virtue, so we all had our own routines during the long hours of curfew - I would use that time to read or make copious notes and plan my schedule for the coming days. Being cooped up in a claustrophobic little office-cum-sleeping space in Mazar-e-Sharif felt no less than living through a daily prison sentence, which not only restricted our movements but also the activities we were permitted to bide our time in the dim light of a kerosene lamp.

The nights were particularly tough in the freezing winter months when the local *bukhari,* or charcoal stove, was the only source of warmth - not ideal for a restful night's sleep for fear of carbon monoxide poisoning. It is perhaps difficult for us to imagine such constraints in an era of ubiquitous charging points, but the few hours of power we did enjoy were hardly enough to charge up our laptops and other devices sufficiently. Along with my colleagues, I learnt crucial skills of frugality and making do with what little was at hand.

Till date, I recall that eerie quiet of the night, broken occasionally only by the sound of some stray gunshots in the distance. I tried to follow the maxim "early to bed, early to rise", but the body clock often refused to cooperate in such alien conditions and there was a lot of unwelcome thinking time to wrestle with on those long, cold and dreary nights. Thoughts about family and loved ones far away triggered bitter-sweet emotions, even as I prayed for the success of my mission. "Help me, please" was how my conversation with God went on those melancholy nights, because the one thing I was certain of was that this was God's work I had been deputed to accomplish.

I was keenly aware of the disconcerting fact that if something untoward were to happen to me out in this curfew-stricken corner of the earth, no one would come to know the full facts – at least not for a very long time. The only connection back home was in the form of a huge, bulky satellite phone which we used sparingly; not only due to the prohibitive $10 per minute cost, but also due to its attraction as a gadget worth grabbing for the local spies who lurked amongst us. In today's world of slick mobile phones and instant connectivity, having to ration our time on such devices to send very brief urgent emails or even a few words of reassurance back home read like such an ancient concept, even to me.

These bulky briefcase-encased satellite phones gradually gave way to chunky mobile phones, which made connectivity somewhat easier but only just. It meant long periods of radio silence during which my family would not hear from me and probably just be praying for the best, relying on the adage that no news is hopefully a sign that all must be well.

Coffee Diplomacy

As a British national, I was also required to register with the local Governor of Mazar-e-Sharif to be allowed to carry on my work in his jurisdiction before we made our journey by road to Pol-e-Khumri – another FOCUS base in the region.

We had an appointment scheduled with Governor Wakil Muttawakil, if I recall his name correctly, and made our way to his non-descript office in good time. I was mindful of the precarious grounds of this meeting, given that it would be conducted via translations from Dari into English by Zabi. Once we had made the awkward introductions, the very first question this stern-looking chieftain asked came as a bit of surprise: "Where is Nairobi?"

The formidable warlord was skimming through my passport and noticed my place of birth and was visibly curious about my very mixed heritage. When I explained that Nairobi was in Kenya, which was in East Africa, his next question was equally unexpected: "So, why aren't you black?" I could see he was genuinely confused at this Kenya-born, brown Muslim man who claimed he was British.

At the same time, as my host, he offered me a drink and I opted for coffee – which would go down in history as the strangest tepid drink I have ever had to consume. The reason lies in the Governor's sheer fascination with my tale as I did my best to succinctly trace the history of South Asians of all faiths and traditions, including Ismailis, migrating from the Indian subcontinent – made up of modern-day India, Pakistan, Bangladesh, Bhutan, Maldives, Nepal and Sri Lanka – to Kenya. He listened with rapt attention as I then went on to explain the colonial heritage that resulted in my British passport. I detailed the travails of the migrating families who used the Monsoon winds for their dhows to transport them from India to Africa, the Governor was mesmerised and keen to know more of this migrant history that took him through the trade in spices and the famous Silk Road. He would be listening to the translations by Zabi but more interested in observing my corresponding expressions to get the complete picture of the history that was clearly all very new to him.

I deftly skipped over the dubious dictatorial landscape of East Africa and the infamous Ugandan dictator Idi Amin who had expelled Indians from the country in the 1970s, many of whom found refuge in the UK and went on to become British – for fear that my Afghan host may take affront at any perceived critique of the Taliban's own authoritarianism. As my narrative was unfolding, I could see my host adding several spoons of coffee followed by heaps of sugar into the small cup he was considerately preparing with his own hands for me. By the time I had completed my story – building a strong case for myself as a British national in an unknown land – the concoction that he had been stirring for what seemed like hours, was finally served. It most certainly remains one of my most memorable drinks – as the strongest and sweetest cup of so-called coffee ever! I, however, had no choice but to consume this peculiar brew with a smile and gratitude to the Governor without whose stamp of approval my activities in the region would never have taken off. There is no doubt that he would have taken it as a personal affront if I had not drained that little cup of all its contents, considering it had been prepared by his very own hands.

Eventually, that unconventional coffee diplomacy paid off and by the end of my narration, the Governor's tone and demeanor had visibly altered, and we were now firmly on friendly terms. I could feel myself relax in that stark setting of a rather oppressive office space, made light only through the growing warmth of our exchange. My host then began to inquire about the kind of humanitarian assistance we were there to provide. I explained our grant remit to provide aid to Internally Displaced Persons (IDPs) who had fled the fighting from other parts of the country to find themselves in makeshift, temporary establishments and also to support water supply and sanitation programmes in Pol-e-Khomri. While in Mazar-e-Sharif, we also intended to offer support to students at the local university with some basic stationery supplies and assistance to carry on their education.

I noticed the Governor's ears prick up at the mention of water and soon he asked if we could fix the water supply to the mosque at the local shrine. Clearly, it would win him brownie points with the locals and even though it wasn't on our agenda, Engineer Kudhus very willingly got to work and was able to sort this out without much trouble. As a result, that meeting proved to be a win-win for all sides – the Governor got the credit for the water supply getting fixed and I got my all-important stamp to carry out the operational work I had been deputed to oversee.

In hindsight, that was a significant and opportune first meeting which paved the way for our work in the entire region. It generated another important result in the form of a letter from the local Governor granting us special permission to take photographs that we required for our water sanitation work in the area. A big exemption in a land where such equipment was forbidden for social purposes. It was the pre-digital days when my trusted camcorder would have to be relied upon for videos and images that would be recorded on tiny cassette tapes, many of which still form part of my collection in London – an antique feature for my grandchildren today, but an essential work tool from the time.

On Our Way...

Fully geared up with the requisite permissions, we set off for Pol-e-Khomri via a stopover at Samangan where we had a water supply facility in place at a local boys' schools. It was a joy seeing the thriving school functioning over two shifts as the locals rushed to grab us treats of *quroot* – a local dairy-based delicacy that is particularly associated with that province of Afghanistan. I remember this as a very happy stopover as we met the headteacher, who expressed much gratitude for our organisation's helping hand. The smiling faces of those schoolboys are among my abiding memories from those early days of humanitarian work.

But we had to rush things through to get to our final destination in time before the 1600 curfew. Wherever we were on the road, the overriding thought at the back of my mind was always about ensuring that we must be back at base in time for the curfew! It was a kind of fear of the unknown because we hadn't yet encountered such a situation where we were caught out, but I certainly did not want to find out the consequences the hard way.

With officers of the Ministry of Vice and Virtue out on the streets with whips to crack down on anyone out and about during times of prayer, the sense of foreboding was never far from our minds in any case. Of course, foreigners - visibly so in their western outfits - were exempt from the strict religious diktats but then I did not have that visible exemption to fall back upon. The urgency of ensuring I was indoors and out of direct Taliban scrutiny as soon as the *Azan* (call to prayer) was sounded by the muezzin of the local mosque, became a canny survival instinct. It mirrored the reactions of the locals, as shopkeepers would instantly rush off to the mosque, not concerned about leaving their wares unmonitored because the fear of harsh reprisals from any of the fierce officials on duty meant no one dared even contemplate petty crimes such as shoplifting and theft.

Forcing people to witness public executions on the streets was certainly one effective form of deterrent deployed by the Taliban in those days. I would often hear about men or women who committed adultery being shot or hanged in the town squares, with crowds gathered to watch this gruesome punishment in action.

Internal Fissures

Pol-e-Khomri was a region of very mixed ethnicities, including a substantial presence of the Hazara ethnic group. As Shias, they were persecuted by the Taliban – who tend to be largely Pashtuns (Sunnis). Once the Taliban took over, the Shias faced greater persecution, and the internal fissures became sharper.

For AKDN work, we had staff of all hues as we very consciously appointed workers based on merit, irrespective of their religious affiliation. However, these deep underlying divisions were the ground reality that we had to be mindful of. The Taliban may have been in charge but the power struggles involving local warlords from different tribes – be it Ahmad Shah Masoud who hailed from the Panjshir Valley of northern Afghanistan or Abdul Rashid Dostum who was Uzbek or numerous other lesser-known military chieftains – created a scenario of constantly heightened tensions in the region.

Against this powder keg setting, there was a palpable sense that things could flare up at any moment, with any one or more of these warlords deciding to mount an attack to assert their authority and throw down the gauntlet to the Taliban. With the ubiquitous presence of guns, every village or cluster of villages had their own commander loyal to a chosen warlord with troops under their command. The vision of almost every adult male walking around with Kalashnikov rifles slung around their shoulders, much like the laptop bags we are now familiar with in the western world, remains embedded in my mind's eye to this day. There were no regulations for possessing firearms, as a result of which every other man brandished one – some as an accessory of choice and a symbol of bravado, others for self-preservation.

This volatile political landscape formed the backdrop of our humanitarian mission, which I came to understand well – mainly to ensure that it did not hinder the work we were there to execute, which was to help those displaced within this expansive and fraught battleground. FOCUS remained defiantly neutral and focused on our goals within this highly charged and weaponised landscape.

It was in the interest of the warlords to ensure our work carried on unencumbered because it ensured access to basic supplies and amenities for the locals, whose loyalty they could then rely upon for the longevity of their stronghold in the area. Many of them were in fact quite proactive in identifying the needs of their population and seek out the aid being delivered by FOCUS Humanitarian Assistance.

Ground Assessments

Our office base in Pol-e-Khomri was a luxury compared to the cubbyhole we had left behind in Mazar-e-Sharif, with the grass in its garden pruned in the form of our FOCUS logo - a moving visual reminder of our wider mission of serving people in need by reducing their dependence on humanitarian aid and facilitating their transition to sustainable, self-reliant, and long-term development.

The discussions we would have once it was curfew time, as there wasn't much else to do with the electricity off, proved a great source of learning for me. One of our local staff doubled up as a cook and the food was simple but wholesome, with beans or lentil curry on the menu most nights. Just before the curfew hit, among the daily tasks was for one of our workers to motorbike into town to bring in warm *naan* (flat bread) for our meal. The secret behind his magical ability to keep that bread warm even in the peak of winter for the duration of the ride was also something I learnt during one of these nightly discussions - turns out we were being treated to his armpit-warmed bread, that made the 10-minute journey through the cold secure under his jacket sleeves. These were some light-hearted moments that warmed our hearts on those freezing nights, as we all had a good laugh at my surprise at first hearing about this inventive technique familiar to the locals.

My work on the ground broadly revolved around Vulnerability Analysis and Mapping (VAM) - a core area of the United Nations' World Food Programme (WFP) - providing the basis for most humanitarian work in the region. In fact, I was credited in one of the numerous WFP VAM reports prepared at the time for its in-depth first-hand accounts. These shared assessments, which I take great pride in, were devised with the help of valuable local inputs. Therefore, politics aside, we had a laser focus on identifying the pressing needs of the most vulnerable groups in all parts of the country where we had logistics bases. These draft assessments would then define the course of the assistance that would be deployed based on our response capacity, funding and in-kind donations.

My to-do list was a lengthy one, as I went about collecting the data, identifying the players, holding discussions with the staff on the ground, identifying any gaps, defining clear access points and assessing the security requirements. I would be out in the fields with the clipboard, making assessments of the quantity of food required, transportation and logistics, identifying distribution points and storage needs for the lentils, rice, oil and wheat flour that were to be offered as part of the food programme. Our set-up operated with a handful of permanent staff, with casual labour to be brought on board at the time of distribution.

In Pol-e-Khomri, most of our beneficiaries were IDPs who had fled another part of the country for security or economic reasons and were now trying to build a new life from scratch. These were families in dire need, with many female-headed households with no male breadwinners. Interacting with these IDPs was a moving experience, deeply rooted in the culture of the region. People were not often very forthcoming or communicative but gradually we could feel a bond develop as they realised we were there to help solve some of their very basic problems. Slowly, but surely, we built those all-important human connections for these distressed families to start trusting us with the information that was required and proffer valuable insights.

Frugal Engineering

Potable water supply was among the topmost priorities in a district like Pol-e-Khomri and the wider Baghlan province, where it was a scarcity, and that is where some good old frugal engineering came into play. The mountainous terrain of Afghanistan was home to many freshwater springs and the eye of these springs became our starting point to bypass the need for pumps or generators or a guaranteed electricity supply – resources not easily accessible in the province. Our water engineer would do the reconnaissance including a taste test, and then work out the water supply process with the use of gravity. He designed a system for the water to flow down the slopes into a reservoir or tank and then be led into the villages through pipes on to a common tap, where the residents could fill up their buckets and utensils. This provided the safest and most reliable source of clean water, circumventing the need for any complex engineering works or hygiene treatments, given nature's bounty and the purity of the spring water source.

It was during some of these explorations that we would find ourselves surrounded by a curious bunch of locals keen to find out what's in store for them. There would be a flurry of questions as they eyed my camera furtively, until I produced my photography pass granted by the Governor.

Those moments of sitting down with the local community and listening to their needs were some of the highlights of the ground assessment tours to these far-flung areas of severe deprivation. Despite their daily hardships, I met some of the most hospitable people on this first visit to Afghanistan. They may have had torn shoes on their feet, but their faces shone with smiles as they greeted us out in the fields. They would often invite our team back to their homes for a cup of tea once it became clear to them that we were there to try and transform their lives for the better, even as they tried to build a life for themselves in crumbling buildings abandoned by previous occupants who had fled one of several outbreaks of violence.

The burqa-clad women folk were always on the fringes of such interactions, reflective of the patriarchal power dynamics at play.

On one of our site visits, I recall a curious encounter involving a staff member, originally from Pol-e-Khomri but who had left the city as a child and eventually moved to the US before circling back to his roots in an effort to make a difference. Suddenly, one of the elders among the group who had gathered around us as we conducted our assessment pointed to him and asked if he was the son of a particular gentleman – turns out he was referring to a "wanted man" who had fled the area many years ago. Clearly, while the man's family had fled the country for fear of persecution, the country of his birth had left an indelible mark on his facial features. We all knew the staffer's instant denial of that familial connection was the customary response in such a scenario of shifting loyalties, where the battle lines are so fraught and ever-changing that no one dare reveal their true identity for fear of reprisals – irrespective of the length of time that had elapsed. For those of us witnessing that uncomfortable exchange from the sidelines, the encounter was a stark reminder of the shaky political ground on which we were operating.

So, this first 10-day visit to Afghanistan proved to be a real eye-opener for me on several fronts. The challenges were countless, the terrain difficult, but there was also a sense of coming to grips with the enormous task at hand. Negotiating with the village chiefs and on-boarding the local workers gave me a very well-rounded view of the next steps. I felt quite optimistic and energised by the commitment shown by the local staff. We had accomplished the first major step of matching the supplies with local needs, and now it was down to the distribution.

Home Turf

It was time for my UN flight back to Islamabad. The emotions on this return flight were markedly different from when I had first landed. I felt safer, perhaps the kind of false sense of security that sets in as the fear of the unknown recedes to a certain degree. I was now accustomed to the ways of this conflict-prone region, where gunshots ringing out through the night were the expected ambient noise to fall asleep to. So much so, that as we were driving out of Pol-e-Khomri, we seemed to be driving towards gunshots that were distinctly growing louder with each mile. There were some anxious moments as we wondered exactly what we were headed towards. Eventually, as it seemed to quieten down, our driver quite nonchalantly declared that it must have been part of a local wedding celebration. To this day I remain unsure if he was trying to calm our collective nerves or genuinely believed this reasoning based on his local knowhow of the varying forms and frequencies of the regular firing exercises in the province. It brought into sharp focus the fact that for the residents, these shots no longer denoted imminent danger because guns were so much a part of their daily existence, used as much in celebration as for wreaking havoc.

Once back in Islamabad and after some important debrief sessions, it was finally time for my first homecoming – with my wife and children waiting for me excitedly. Little did we know that soon after I unpacked my bags, I would be getting a call from the head office to make my way to my next mission, which was in Mozambique. (More on that in one of the chapters further down.)

I just about had time to present the family with little cricket souvenirs and keepsakes from Islamabad, including a semi-precious stone-studded map of Afghanistan which still has pride of place in our London flat after all these years of a nomadic existence. But soon it was time to say my goodbyes to them again.

Back in Time

Meanwhile, within a few months of that very first tour as Project Manager in Afghanistan, I was to return to the country – this time to Badakshan and in complete contrast to the first rather smooth journey, in hindsight.

I had to make my way first to Khorog in Tajikistan, neighbouring Afghan Badakshan. This involved a flight from London to Uzbekistan, from where I was driven to Khujand (Tajikistan) – known as Leninabad in the past – to then board a flight to the Tajik capital of Dushanbe. This was followed by a 14 to 16-hour drive to Khorog through the mountain passes.

These road journeys were coordinated between different humanitarian agencies to make them most efficient, given the risky terrain we were to be driven through – prone to avalanches and rock falls. The option of a 45-minute flight was often hampered due to the risky landscape, as planes would have to manoeuvre their way between two peaks to land on a rather obscure runway. Such tricky manoeuvres were inevitably ruled out quite often due to cloudy conditions, leaving the lengthy road trip the most reliable option across the vast expanse of mountainous terrain from Dushanbe to Khorog. It was a tough landscape in more ways than one, with unfamiliar local dialects and hardly any English speakers. I gradually began to identify some familiar words which had their roots in Persian from my previous visit to Tajikistan.

As we headed out of Dushanbe, the first 40-50 kilometers of smooth roads started giving way to the more treacherous hilly terrain. That said, I do believe it's the kind of journey that we would all feel fortunate to make at least once in our lifetime. The pristine natural beauty, especially given the spring greenery and flowers at that time of the year in April 2000, and snow-peaked mountains in view that I encountered on those long road trips have certainly left an indelible mark on my memory.

I could have done without the sole audio cassette of mixed music – including a few Bollywood melodies, some local tunes blended with English pop music – that my driver was clearly very attached to. After its umpteenth loop, I was conscious that each bit of the lyrics had involuntarily embedded in my memory. It added to the sense of monotony that eventually creeps in after the novelty of the exquisiteness of the landscape had worn off many, many hours into the journey.

We passed through tiny hamlets lined with mud houses, taking in rest stops to refuel and some impromptu, and rather quite amusing, car washes facilitated by natural springs along the way. I soon became familiar with the quirks of the local area, where broken down cars would stay stalled in the middle of the road rather than make an effort to be pushed out of the way to the side of the narrow road. My driver explained in his broken English that this was to ensure that the next vehicle on the road would be forced to stop and assist the stranded driver, instead of just callously driving past.

There was also a handy barter system at play between these resourceful people. After my driver ran into a home on the way when he was low on fuel to come back with a large can of petrol, I enquired how much that urgent pit stop had cost him. He casually responded to say "nothing" because the next time that friend visits Dushanbe, this fuel favour would be reimbursed in kind. Local problems, local solutions, I thought!

The warmth of the soup, or *chorba* as the locals called it, on the *Chai Khana* (tea-food) stops on this long and winding road trip brings back some warm memories to this day. The friendly locals were often keen to know more about this foreigner from London; "do you know my cousin in Germany?" asked one friendly restauranteur with a beaming smile. For them, Europe was one homogenous mass where they expected everyone was known to each other to a certain degree. *Yuk pyala chai,* or one cup of tea, was the offer with which they always greeted their guests, which was never just one cup but encompassed several cups of tea, cakes, savoury delicacies and lots of warm chatter.

In Khorog, this warmth extended to a hearty Indian meal at a restaurant named Delhi Durbar – run by a Tajik married to an Indian, cooking up a delicious mix of spices and flavours.

Review and Analysis

My reason to visit Tajikistan was two-fold – one, as a familiarisation tour of accessing Afghan Badakshan across the border and the second reason was to facilitate the visit of an independent evaluator whose sign-off would be critical for the successful implementation of our development plans in the region.

The Canadian government was the donor and FOCUS Canada had facilitated the tour of an evaluator named Robert Vandenburgh (Bob), who would be conducting the analysis and also advising us on the second grant we were in the process of applying for. He was accompanied by two members of the board of FOCUS Canada, conducting a site visit for an overview of these plans.

I initially made my way to the Kyrgyzstan city of Osh, where the FOCUS procurement hub was located. All the food supplies coming in from the US or sourced from around other parts of the region would be stored here and then trucked down as required to Tajikistan from where it was loaded on to dinghies to make the river crossing over to the Afghan side for distribution among the vulnerable families.

These essential food supplies were based on the World Food Programme's standard distribution guidelines for humanitarian assistance, determined by each area's staple diet. For example, a family of six in Afghanistan would be entitled to a 50kg bag of flour along with other cooking essentials such as oil and lentils to make up a standard food basket. The number of food baskets to be distributed in a year was determined by the assessment of the needs and requirements of these families.

The purpose of the evaluation visit at this stage was to review how things were operating at the procurement hub at Osh from an audit point of view, on behalf of the Canadian authorities behind the grant funding for the initiative. The food essentials acquired through this grant would then have the requisite clearance to be stamped as donated by the Canadian government.

My task was to conduct a review at Osh, collect documents and take photographic evidence that would provide an overview of our operations to the visiting team. I then took the short flight from Osh to Bishkek (capital of Kyrgyzstan), where the Canadian team was waiting for me to escort them over to Khorog – another journey that would leave an indelible mark on my memory.

One of our local operatives in Bishkek, Talaant, was working on getting us tickets on a commercial flight to Dushanbe (Tajikistan) for the first leg of this journey. It soon became apparent that getting four seats on the flight was unlikely, but he knew that it was imperative for us to travel together as a team. So, in another classic display of local problems being solved with local solutions, the resourceful Talaant indicated to me in his broken English to remain within the terminal complex. I could tell he had a scheme up his sleeve to make this journey happen for us, having pocketed a large wad of cash towards the ticketing arrangements. After much uncertainty, it transpired that two of the four seats were now confirmed. Despite a shortfall of two seats, he confidently asked all four of us to follow him outside the bounds of the terminal onto the tarmac, bypassing any customary check in or passport control processes. As we edged closer to a waiting aircraft, a security guard discreetly opened a side gate to let us through.

There it was – the Yak-40 aircraft that would be flying us to Dushanbe with the steps leading up to the cabin, or so I thought. But it soon became obvious through gestures and rudimentary English that only two of us would be travelling in the passenger cabin, with my colleague, Noor, and I destined for the luggage hold of the plane! I chose to share only part of this information with my co-passengers, ambiguously ushering Bob, the evaluator, and another colleague, Shiraz, towards their seats with a promise to catch up with them a little later. The 40-seater plane was soon packed to the very last seat, leaving the two of us along with two air stewardesses hanging on for dear life in the luggage hold as the captain prepared for takeoff.

The lights went off as we precariously perched on some sturdy-looking but far from stable suitcases. The very nonchalant approach of the air stewardesses offered a sense of comfort as it implied that this was not such an unusual way to fly in this part of the world, after all. Looking back, I can see the funny side of this takeoff that broke all aviation codes and safety protocols but at the time I am sure I had some misgivings – most of which have now faded into the background as the achievements on the ground stand the test of time.

Now, I just remember laughing along with Noor, reassured by the casual tea-making of the stewardesses as they went about their flight duties. Having previously travelled on a flight more akin to an air-taxi with passengers standing to make room for their bag of potatoes, being accommodated in the luggage hold was far less of a shock than it would have been under other circumstances. *(As an aside, more about that absurd air-taxi flight to come in the Conclusion!)*

Crossing Points

After the unconventional flight and a 14-hour car journey from Dushanbe, we finally arrived in Khorog to get our work started, addressing the many questions the evaluator had to analyse if our assessments on paper matched up with the realities on the ground to ensure the smooth progress of the mission. We set off by familiarising him with the vast geographical spread, bordered by the River Panj - also known as the Oxus or Amu Darya - and the dozen crossing points for the aid to make its way to Afghanistan that we had negotiated with the local chieftains of the region. Our advance team had completed the assessment of the cluster of villages around each of these points.

After pinpointing these clusters on the map, the evaluator chose a few of them at random for his review and shortlisted around a dozen families for a kind of snap inspection of the humanitarian assistance received from FOCUS recently. These were vulnerable poverty-stricken families, suffering in the aftermath of a drought and also isolated within their own country, given the harsh mountainous terrain. The arable land being scarce, any local food production was barely enough to sustain even a fraction of the population of the village despite their well-oiled barter system. Once our supply trucks arrived at the crossing points, the villagers would gather across the river to meet the boatloads of food supplies, which were then distributed based on the needs of the individual households.

Once again, local problems being solved by local solutions was in action as the inhabitants learnt to master the many moody tides of the river. The crossing points were chosen with care to ensure the food trucks could be brought close to the water's edge for offloading. An arrow would be tied to the end of a fishing line with one end of a rope and then shot across to the other side of the river, where the villagers would grab the end of the line with the rope which they then securely fastened to a sturdy tree or rock. This created a kind of safety harness for the rubber dinghy loaded with supplies, with the rope used as protection against the rapid currents of the river dragging the dinghies astray, thus enabling the food consignments safely across choppy waters to the Afghan side. The rowers then manoeuvred their precious cargo with this rope trick to keep the boats in line – quite literally. Local problems, local solutions!

Over time, of course, I witnessed the process transform as we built a bridge over the river – a heartening change that made life just that little bit easier for the vulnerable families.

Horse Ride to Remember

During that particular visit, our boat, or rather inflatable dinghy, was packed with essentials and mercifully the river was calm enough to avoid the need for this innovative rope technique. Besides our little group, we also had a customs official accompanying us on the dinghy to cross the river with us and stamp our passports to legitimise our crossing over into a foreign land – from Tajikistan to Afghanistan.

It was a stark reminder that the river border was born out of arbitrary man-made decisions to demarcate a landscape that was essentially one. However, arbitrary or not, we had to be armed with multiple entry visas to ensure we did not get caught out at the check points on either side. As a result, the customs officer was quite accustomed to being ferried back and forth several times across the river for this purpose. One couldn't help but lament the pointlessness of such artificial divides, but crucial humanitarian interventions had to carry on regardless.

It was soon time for yet another precarious journey, this time on horseback deep into the mountainous terrain to access the village clusters ear-marked for the evaluation. We walked across the dirt tracks on the other side of the river, passing by a few shops selling some basics like tea, sugar, oil and soap in a handful of wooden shacks that passed off as the local bazaar. This 'bazaar' is where we hired the horses that would transport us up the mountain passes of the Pamir Range via extremely narrow donkey tracks. The width of these tracks was such that as we trod along the path one shoulder would graze the side of the mountain, even as the horse veered dangerously close to the edge on the other side – a sheer drop to certain death.

Those narrow brushes with death, during which I was torn between whether to hold on to my horse's reins tighter or loosely as the best life-saving technique, certainly made this a horse-ride to remember. For a novice with no training and only ever having experienced horse-riding as a kid on some fun seaside holidays, this was a naturally scary escapade with the reins of your life quite literally in your own hands. Safe to say, I had no temptation to enact scenes out of my favourite Hollywood Country Westerns and try out any galloping across those mountain passes. There was no such heroism on my mind; I simply averted my gaze away from the deathly drop and hoped for the best as the owner of the horses led our convoy of unskilled horse riders. Every member of our party probably had similar misgivings racing through their minds, but no one uttered any words of complaint; after all, this was the job we had all signed up for.

We finally arrived at our destination of Weir village, where the locals had been expecting us with a very welcome cup of warm tea. My Programme Manager had warned me that there would be no electricity or basic amenities such as running water or toilets where we were headed. Therefore, we had two options for our morning toilet run – to join the local gossip gang that gathered daily for a communal squat, while also catching up on the latest village goings on, or head out to the fields solo. I chose the latter, largely because I knew I would not have much to contribute to the local gossip. But I felt quite privileged to have been offered the option to be treated as one of the locals, even though I did not speak their language. I am quite certain the foreign influx of us strangers would have featured heavily on the day's gossip agenda!

Hand of God

While in the village, we were welcomed into one of the homes selected at random by the evaluator for his inspection. We had to crouch down to enter this mud tenement, which was essentially an open space artificially demarcated into a kitchen and seating area, devoid of any form of furniture. There were no windows in this home because in the winters the only way they could shield themselves from the sub-zero temperatures would be by sealing the one opening, which was their main door.

We all joined them on a worn-out rug on the floor for the discussions, moderated by our local translator. I spotted the FOCUS food basket delivery of a bag of wheat and oil and felt reassured that all seemed to be working as it should on the ground. The evaluator set about checking off his list of questions through the translator as I silently prayed that everything matches up, as it should – name, number of family members, the amount of ration they consume and the amount they use for barter.

Within the local barter economy, there is a leeway in humanitarian assistance for this adjustment because it allows the locals to exchange a small part of their food essentials with small "luxuries" – such as tea or sugar, things that would hardly qualify as luxury items in non-conflict zones. If this barter amount was over the acceptable percentage, it would reflect a discrepancy in the need analysed for that particular cluster of villages.

However, thankfully, all the details tallied with our records, and everyone was well below the barter threshold. But the process of getting that information was a bit of a sensitive one, with the beneficiary seeming visibly upset on being questioned about it. The translator managed the situation diplomatically but later explained to me privately that the reason for his agitation was that for him and his family, that food basket was a gift from their Imam, and they would not even dream of exchanging such a divine gift.

That was a very moving experience for me, to note that to them it was irrelevant whether the source of that assistance was in Canada or elsewhere. Ultimately, they viewed it as a gift from God and that is how they treated what they saw as a holy bounty. It reflected the strength of their faith; to them the Imam was the divine hand sheltering them and showering gifts from God. It shone a light on their unshakeable belief system, which gave them the hope and courage to survive in such a harsh terrain. That hope gave them the much-needed sense of not being alone in their daily struggles because God was watching over them, always.

The Great Game

The evaluation complete, it was time to head towards the wooden structure prepared by the head of the village for us to tuck ourselves into our sleeping bags. Perched high up at the village of Weir in pitch dark, I could see the bright lights of Khorog on the other side sparkling in the night and the hustle and bustle of cars.

It made me ruminate about how politics creates such unnecessary divides, with people of neighbouring villages speaking the same Shughni dialect of the Dari language split up arbitrarily in the Great Game of politics – while one side of that divide flourishes with all the modern amenities, the other side where we had sought our nightly refuge struggled to eke out a very basic existence. The sheer unfairness and futility of war struck me like a sharp bolt that night!

It was apparent that Western superpowers dictated the destinies of these innocent people all over the continent, fighting over the resources and carving out land without much thought for the human lives at stake. Much of these thoughts travelled with me downhill on our way back, a relatively easier journey than the precarious one on the way into the village - battling through rockslides and horse tantrums along the way. We headed off after some delicious freshly baked bread, honey and green tea thanks to our generous hosts, pooled in by the villagers happy to share whatever little they had with their foreign visitors.

That was one village cluster down, followed by three more clusters shortlisted for the evaluation, including one where the distribution process was underway at the village of Yak Daru - which roughly translates as "the first village on the river". There we came across an over-enthusiastic village head who readily agreed to be filmed on camera to express his gratitude to the donors, whom we explained were the taxpayers of Canada. However, in his excitement on camera, we had to go through several takes as he kept repeating the line: "I would like to thank the Islamic government of Canada". When explained by the translator during the course of the successive failed takes that Canada was not an Islamic state, his ultimate response evoked many smiles all round: "Then why are they helping us?"

A perfectly innocent question, which once again reflected the enduring role of faith in their lives and also the selfless acts of countries keen to help in a crisis.

57

Food for Work

With the evaluation successfully completed, our second grant was now guaranteed. It was tied to the World Food Programme's "Food for Work" initiative – which was aimed at meeting the wider self-reliance goals in these areas. It involved the use of local skills to create essential infrastructure such as roads and bridges, backed up by the expertise and support provided by FOCUS.

The ethos of the AKDN and its agencies and affiliates, including FOCUS, has always been centered around self-reliance, with all our initiatives based on the needs identified by the local communities themselves rather than imposed upon them by outsiders. This bottom-up approach lies at the heart of the Aga Khan Rural Support Programme Model, which involved us visiting communities and using food as an instrument of peace in war-ravaged areas. Where there is lack of food, there is conflict and therefore the approach of food for peace yielded promising results on the ground.

We would meet the local village chiefs and explain that in exchange for the food we would be offering them, we can deploy their abundant local skills to help build and create whatever is the most pressing needs of the local community. Some would seek ease of access through some basic transport and others would ask for drinking water supply. FOCUS would provide the engineering, and the local residents would provide the labour, who would then be remunerated with food. As a result, what we were able to deliver was a community asset that would not only provide long-lasting benefits to the community but also something they could take pride in as their own creation. We would always insist on a participatory approach, preferably involving the women of the communities to get a different perspective because women always kept the needs of the whole family at the forefront. It ensured the right balance in the decision-making process, which often involved a very basic planning system using a tree branch as a marker and the sandy ground as an ideas board.

As an interesting aside, I recall how one well-meaning international humanitarian agency observed the hardship faced by the women folk of a particular village as they trudged for miles twice a day to the river to access the day's drinking water supply for their home while the men folk were working in the fields. It not only took up a lot of time but also meant the women carrying heavy pots of water back and forth. The agency decided that digging a well for this village would be the most useful investment for the community. However, it was only once this good deed was completed that it emerged that the women folk were extremely unhappy with this new well as it had taken away their only daily social outing. Once freed up from the walks to the river and back, the men folk expected them to start lending a hand in the fields – leaving them with no time to themselves amid their other household chores. The discontent was soon smoothened over by the agency with some good diplomacy and alternative income generating schemes in the form of a biogas project. This involved the women collecting cattle manure that provided a sustainable source of cooking fuel, with the residual ashes converted to fertilizer – a good source of employment and income for the women folk.

While the agency that shall remain unnamed did manage to turn things around, for us this experience was an important reminder, and indeed a lesson, about the importance of consultation with the community before initiating any new project intended for their benefit. The outcome of these dialogues was assets that would survive the test of time, with schools, clinics and shops kick-starting the local economy and offering choices to families, including to send girls to school to be educated. Rudimentary roads replaced the dirt tracks and eventually the cluster of villages had some road connectivity, facilitated using dynamite to blast through the mountains.

It was all done manually through painstaking hard work of the villagers, with engineering support and food provided by us. FOCUS was coordinating the grants, with the entire amount going towards the Food for Work initiative because all the administrative costs were covered by us. It made us the favoured partners on the ground, with agencies comfortable in the knowledge that 100 per cent of the grant funds were being deployed towards humanitarian assistance to those most in need.

Bridge to the Future

While I continued to make several trips back and forth to the region, it was around two years later that I was to return to the very spot in Weir village where I had experienced the scariest horse-ride of my life. Now, before me was an entirely transformed local community.

The rickety dinghy ride across the river had given way to a fairly smooth car journey across a fully functional bridge. Instead of walking up a dirt track to the nearest "bazaar" to acquire horses for the onward journey, we were driven up to a proper marketplace – no longer just a few basic wooden shacks, but a whole range of quite large shops selling anything and everything, from clothes to cosmetics.

Wow! What a change a little helping hand for better connectivity can make to a village, I remember thinking. The sense of joy and satisfaction I felt in my heart at that moment resonates till today. Of course, the roads through the mountain pass would be shut during the peak winter months but during the summer months it had created the kind of hustle and bustle that was unimaginable during my very first evaluation visit in 2000. Back then, people around there had never had the chance to touch a car, let alone ride in one. Now, all of that was in the past and this was their new reality.

Goods were now finding their way from China through Tajikistan across the bridge and the mountain pass all the way to Kabul, from where goods from Pakistan would make their way back into these Afghan villages. These hamlets had their own pop-up markets up and running, which sold their local produce at trade fairs organised on either side of the bridge every alternate month. A customs office, created at the same time as the bridge connecting Tajikistan and Afghanistan on the river border was being built, facilitated the smooth transit of these traders on either side to make the journey. This flourishing trade had injected life into the communities, which was heartening to witness.

Later, I would return to Khorog around four-five years down the line and discover that a hydroelectricity plant, Pamir Energy, had brought electricity across the river in the village of Weir where I had spent a memorable inspection night. The head of the plant, Daler, offered to take me out to dinner to Delhi Durbar – my cherished Indian restaurant – and later for a drive along the river towards the bridge and parked up. I looked across with blurry eyes that had welled up with tears as I could see bright shining lights in Weir that had been cloaked in total darkness only a few years ago. Daler joked how he had brought me on a sightseeing tour of the "Las Vegas of the Shugnan region". I could feel a deep sense of gratification wash over me as I experienced one of my many wondrous realisations of darkness giving way to light and despair giving way to hope.

Post-Taliban Landscape

As someone who was to become deeply acquainted with this region and its terrain, my return to Afghanistan in the wake of the 11 September 2001 terrorist attacks presented a stark contrast to the Taliban-dominated political scenario of the past.

Given our successful track record of utilising food as an instrument for peace and creating community-driven assets in the region, AKDN was among the first agencies asked to step in for humanitarian relief and reconstruction work in the wake of the US-led military operation ousting the Taliban and to coordinate with the new President Hamid Karzai led government. It was a massive commitment by AKDN at the time. We had the infrastructure in place, so the focus now would be on building on it from a reconstruction perspective even as the immediate relief work remained ongoing.

We knew we were stepping into a very delicate situation in the immediate aftermath of the war. The Taliban had been defeated but hadn't disappeared overnight, which meant that factional fighting and ongoing gun fights between warring factions were very much the norm as I landed in November 2001.

I was part of a large delegation flying in on a UN flight via Pakistan to assess requirements on the ground, with members of the group heading out to different regions of Afghanistan. My group landed at an airport near Kabul where the American troops were stationed and set off for Kabul by road. We were all looking forward to a bite to eat at the end of a long journey and as we drove into the Afghan capital, I was accosted with a very drastically transformed city from my previous visits. Gone were the Taliban imposed restrictions, the streets were abuzz with activity and there was even music blaring in the restaurant we chose. While some armed American troops patrolled the streets in a peacekeeping capacity, the general ambience was one of jubilation and a sense of freedom.

It was very visibly apparent that the days of long beards, restricted socialising, curfews and lashings by the Ministry of Vice and Virtue for small transgressions were a thing of the past. There were more women out and about as well, though also some begging on the streets for alms. This was a totally different Afghanistan and the nature of our assistance work also underwent a change – eventually making AKDN not only the highest taxpayers but also the largest employer of women in the region.

However, the fragile stability that characterised the Taliban domination was also transformed in the process by a much more uncertain and unpredictable set of local power dynamics. We were very aware that we must proceed with utmost caution. Our group of 25-30 officials and experts soon split up to head to different regions and my group was destined for Bamiyan – by now a very well-known Afghan city since it hit worldwide headlines for the 6th century monumental statues of Buddha carved on the side of a cliff that had been smashed to smithereens for being "un-Islamic" by the Taliban in March 2001.

Close Shave with Death

My task was to set up a FOCUS office in Bamiyan and this initial visit was a reconnaissance mission towards that end, to create a base for humanitarian and eventually reconstruction work for the region. But getting there proved quite a precarious undertaking. We were camped out at our offices in Pol-e-Khumri and were made aware of some skirmishes which meant we could not fly out immediately to Bamiyan. Once we had the clearance to travel, my group gathered in the mud patch with goal posts that served as the local football field to be airlifted by a government helicopter.

As we waited for our ride, we noticed some armed Afghan men gathering on the hills above us, possibly gearing up for an attack to take charge of Pol-e-Khomri. The sense of dread at that moment sends shivers down my spine even today as perhaps one of the closest shaves with death I had. One of our operatives equipped with a satellite phone was in communication with the base of the helicopter operations to give them a heads up of this imminent attack. They had intelligence of this looming conflict in Pol-i-Khomri but stressed that they were on the way to get us out of there. All the while, we could see that we were being boxed in by the local warriors atop the hill and soon decided to abandon the idea of getting out to Bamiyan that day. But just as we headed to our cars to be driven back to base, we heard the first gun shots being fired. While there was no way of knowing if these shots were aimed at us or a warring faction nearby, what was certain at the point was that we were now very much caught in the middle of a serious clash.

Amidst the firing, we were relieved to hear what sounded like a chopper heading our way. Our satellite phone operative was being given instructions for us to jump in as it got closer to the ground because it did not plan to land or switch off the engines, given the war-like scenario and gun battle that was unfolding. I couldn't help but recall scenes from some of those high-octane Hollywood thrillers where the star of the film makes death-defying helicopter escapes – 'Mission Impossible' style! Here we were a group of simple humanitarian workers shielding our eyes from the dust flying all around as the helicopter propellers edged closer towards the football field and we all threw in our belongings and jumped in one by one, with gunshots still flying all around us.

In hindsight, I can see the light-hearted cinematic side of this brush with death but at that moment in time the daring getaway felt anything like a filmy scenario.

Buddhas of Bamiyan

As we landed, the first sight I witnessed were the cavernous holes which once housed the exotic Buddhas. Not only that, I also spotted the unexploded missiles used to blow up these iconic monuments and empty bullet shells strewn all over the ground. I was overcome by a sense of loss at this ancient piece of history being blasted off in such a callous manner. What a loss to humanity! I recall feeling quite bereft as I thought this has got nothing to do with religion, this is not Islamic in any way. We as Muslims know this is not Islam, which stands for peace among all faiths. Our organisation works towards preserving cultural heritage for the future generations but when it comes to an act like this, what will the future generations think of our generation that oversaw such thoughtless destruction. This was the sense of disquiet that I was overcome with on landing in Bamiyan. At the same time, there was also a very vulnerable feeling knowing that we had just landed in some very volatile territory.

Our first task was to approach the Governor of Bamiyan to get to our government-approved accommodation. It was a huge relief when the Governor turned out to be a very generous and hospitable man. With his help, we began work to set up a base and started conducting reviews of the local needs of the villagers. We had to travel through heavy snow in freezing temperatures, which impacted visibility as we drove through the villages and would often be on foot to get to the remote areas. Our group encountered some of the most vulnerable families on these treacherous journeys. They were, however, filled with warmth and hospitality at the same time - offering us the succour of tea in the harsh cold. These families were sustaining themselves on limited supplies of dried fruit and were fast running out of supplies.

On our reconnaissance missions, we heard that there were IDPs sheltering within the caves that once housed the Buddhas and decided to check this information out. And lo and behold, there were families sheltering from the December cold in those caves. They were keeping warm with small fires that had created hazardous smoke within the enclosed space without any ventilation. As we filmed for our inspection, I remember the coughing all around as those fires were made up of anything and everything they could find - not necessarily just wood.

I was deeply moved and overcome with emotion when I witnessed this scene. I couldn't help wondering what if these were my children shivering to keep warm in a smoke-filled cave? But in our line of work, we do need to learn to suppress our emotions and be professional to be able to help these vulnerable families. I had to reassure myself that I was in a position to do something for them. One of our first actions after this was to tell the local Governor that we would start by assisting the families in these caves - shoes for children, warm clothing and some blankets as a start. We were able to action this quite quickly and get the supplies to them straight away.

This completed the first phase of that visit during which we were able to meet the immediate needs and establish a base in Bamiyan for future activities in support of the community. I had a chance to return home to London briefly and undertake further assessments with the team and finetune the proposals. I returned to Bamiyan after a short hiatus with AKDN's sectoral experts on education, health and agriculture. I was asked to step in at the last-minute when the leader of this mission, Najmi, was incapacitated by a painful toothache. As someone who knew the region well, I was tasked with guiding this team around and for me it was a great opportunity to oversee FOCUS' humanitarian work transition to the development phase.

While I was the one who knew the terrain well and had local expertise, the others were the real experts. On this particular road trip, we had to cross a very rickety bridge over a deep valley that was a structure made up of planks of wood with no barriers on either side. So, we got off and crossed by foot while the driver crossed with an empty car, praying that the planks of wood don't suddenly snap mid-way. Another scary journey and close brush with death, all in a day's work for me while in this conflict zone and not always to do with war and bullets. The driver had probably been accustomed to this crossing, but we showered him with praise for this feat he accomplished, nonetheless.

As we carried on, two of us took turns to give the driver a break while driving through those icy roads – a journey never to be forgotten, with at least one death-defying swerve that thankfully landed us towards the mountain side of the road and not towards the deep valley.

Looking to the Future

By the time I returned to Kabul in 2002, it was with a longer-term mission to set up a full-fledged office in the Afghan capital at a time when the foreign embassies were opening up again. As an example of how things had massively changed, our rent spiked from $400 a month to $2,500 and that too as a take it or leave it scenario – an indication of a booming economic landscape. This was a country on the move under a legitimate new government and we set up base in the Wazir Akbar Khan neighbourhood of Kabul – the diplomatic enclave in the heart of a resurgent capital city. Our Islamabad and Khorog offices became sub-offices, with Kabul now the main HQ.

I was witnessing a fast pace of change right before my eyes, from war-torn buildings to shopping malls, restaurants and businesses flourishing in Kabul. There was a palpable sense of optimism on the streets and schools were up and running, girls back in classrooms. It was a very welcome new scenario.

During the trip to Bamiyan, we went to meet with the International Committee of the Red Cross (ICRC), which go into disaster zones and exit after the emergency phase. They were running a clinic and asked us to take it over as they prepared to leave but could see that there was still a massive need, even though their emergency camps had to be wrapped up. The training requirements for traditional birth attendants (TBAs) was as high as ever, as were most other medical expertise. With the Taliban being ousted, the demand for these medical services had soared as all sects felt safer to access these services without fear or favour.

Eventually we did take over this clinic, which expanded the scope of the services it provided. Years later it was converted and today it is one the largest hospital and medical training centres in Afghanistan – solar powered, hi-tech and world class. The sense of pride I feel for this Bamiyan Hospital dating back to a small basic clinic in 2002 has outlived all the political upheavals that were yet to come. This is an enduring symbol of the impact on the ground made by FOCUS and AKDN, which starts as a humanitarian effort and then goes on to create a legacy for the region – often against the backdrop of political unrest and turbulence.

If I contrast this with the demolition of the Buddhas, here is an effort to create institutions that can withstand the test of time – at least in our living memory – so that we can show that humanity ultimately can prevail over destruction. And we don't necessarily need branding or plaudits because the ultimate aim is to benefit the local community and create a regional hub of excellence.

In the same vein, while I was setting up our office in Kabul, I had the opportunity to work on what I proudly proclaim as my favourite project in Afghanistan. We got the chance to be a part of what in the development sector is known as Quick Impact Projects (QIPs). The idea was to give some comfort to the local population with initiatives creating visible impact relatively quickly.

Our FOCUS team in Kabul identified a few projects under this QIP scheme: one was for water supply and the other was the Tajwar Sultana Girls School. This school already existed but being a girls' school, it was shut down by the Taliban. Once the old regime had been ousted, the girls had started going back to this school in two shifts – even though this was a mere shell of a building, with a black painted wall serving as a makeshift blackboard.

Under the QIP scheme, we decided to rehabilitate this school and looked for partners to equip the school's library. A FOCUS Canada official wrote to me to say that the Colonel Fred Scott Elementary School and Rotary Club in the country wanted to fundraise for children in Afghanistan and asked me for suggestions. This was a fortuitous intervention, as I instantly offered him the chance to help equip the Tajwar Sultana Girls School library with books. What we got in the end turned out to be funds not only enough for the books but also some computers, making it the first girls' school in the country to have access to these devices. This, along with internet connectivity from our mobile phone initiative in Kabul, opened up a whole new world for those schoolgirls.

The reason for this being my favourite project is that some years down the line, London 2018, I came across a young Afghan woman named Rahila who was working with FOCUS on the resettlement of refugees from conflict affected countries, mainly Afghanistan and Syria. Rahila informed me that she had studied at this school in Kabul and remembered the launch of this library as a little schoolgirl. The sense of joy and pride I felt at this piece of information is quite difficult to encapsulate in mere words.

Looking back at those early precarious flights into Afghanistan at the mercy of daily curfew to landing at a functional airport and being whisked off to a hotel, this thriving new country finding its feet held out a lot of promise. Meeting young employees that I had recruited as junior staffers and to see them now flourishing as senior executives gave me a strong sense of accomplishment and reiterated the broader mission we undertake – of making a small difference in the lives of innocent people engulfed by conflict and strife.

Earthquake Relief

In 2002, aside from my regular duties, I happened to be in London for meetings when news of the earthquake in Nahrain, in Baghlan province of Afghanistan, broke around the world. This was not far from Pol-e-Khumri, where we now had our office overseeing an established humanitarian presence.

I was to take along a young volunteer, Akbar, an investment banker turned pilot who was keen to give something back to society. Our relief efforts in the quake-hit territories were to be his first brush with humanitarian work before he was stationed at one of the FOCUS offices.

The orders came in for us to get to Dubai as soon as possible and get ourselves on one of the flights from there on to Kabul. The political landscape had undergone much change and with the Hamid Karzai government having replaced the Taliban, things could work more smoothly. His Highness the Aga Khan had made a commitment to offer additional support required in the aftermath of the natural disaster and given the urgency, we were able to get on board an Afghan C130 military plane that was headed back to Mazar-e-Sharif from Dubai.

On landing, we made our way to Nahrain, where our local team was already at work with organising relief efforts in the immediate aftermath at the camp set up by United Nations Office for the Coordination of Humanitarian Affairs (UNOCHA). This was a massive earthquake, which meant a lot of ground had to be covered to provide support to communities who had lost their homes. With FOCUS already familiar with the local landscape, our team had been asked to assist with the set up and support of a rota with other aid agencies to man the Emergency Operations Centre (EOC) - the centralised location of emergency response and recovery support operations in the wake of natural disasters and other crises. So, by the time we arrived two days after the quake had hit, the FOCUS team had already carved out the kind of support that would be required, including access to food stockpiles from our warehouses not very far off.

Our commitment was to provide the food support, with other agencies covering aspects such as shelter and non-food items, like blankets and other essentials. We also committed to setting up Water Bladders - a very effective hydration system containing a mattress-like reservoir with a capped mouth that can be filled up with water and a hose fitted in for drinking water to be dispensed on the other end. Our water sanitation engineers had been hard at work in the region already, getting fresh-water wells and other techniques of sourcing clean water from springs to be used as potable drinking water. We used some of that expertise to find the "eye of the spring", fill up water tankers from the nearest springs and then drive these down to the affected areas to pump through that water into the Water Bladders, which became the crucial drinking water supply for the displaced families who were able to fill up with the taps located around these makeshift reservoirs.

Meanwhile, from Tajikistan, truckloads of second-hand clothing were making their way to Nahrain, arriving just as we did. These were driven by Russian drivers, who began displaying some rather odd behaviour in refusing to offload the consignment which we were keen to start distributing among the families. It was when I called our AKDN representative in Tajikistan that the reason for this dilly-dally became clearer – the drivers were expecting a bribe, or in the words of our rep, they needed to be introduced to "Benjamin Franklin" i.e. $100 banknotes.

I refused to compromise on this point and went to the UN coordinator to inform them that the supplies are here but getting them offloaded will need some intervention. I have no idea what kind of powers of persuasion they used in the end, but we were finally able to get things moving. Having our office and guest house not too far away in Pol-e-Khomri proved to be a real bonus, as it meant I was able to avoid the pit that had been dug up for use as a communal toilet for all agency workers. I decided a trip to our office and back every few days for a quick freshen up was well worth the trek!

The office also helped provide important sustenance, saving our team from the tasteless military rations provided for all the humanitarian agencies to survive on. We drove our cook down to the tent in Nahrain to cook some food, very basic but at least they were warm meals and not tasteless pre-packaged powder-based mush that was the only alternative. Soon, as word of this spread around the camps, the FOCUS tent became the most popular hangout for all other agency heads during mealtimes.

Another abiding memory of this two-week humanitarian mission to a country I came to know well is of the aftershocks and tremors every so often as we tried to sleep in our sleeping bags on the ground in our tent. These are very frightening indeed, keeping us awake as we prayed for the minor tremors not to intensify into another quake. But things fell into place quite well in the end and the team was able to complete the tasks after I headed back to Kabul.

Fortuitously, while I was there, organisers of a fundraising campaign in London dialled in to us on our satellite phone and I was able to give them a first-hand account of the distress on the ground. I gave the donors a detailed rundown of the work being done and asked for their prayers. I was later told about the very positive impact this direct dial into the disaster zone had on the fundraising efforts, galvanising their efforts on hearing a voice directly from the field about the devastation among the rural communities who had lost their homes and livelihoods. With the humanitarian agencies taking charge of their basic day-to-day requirements of food, water, shelter and some essential clothing, these displaced families were slowly able to focus on rebuilding their lives – bit by bit.

My last visit to Afghanistan would have been around 2008 and since then observing the turmoil of the recent years with the return of the Taliban has been harrowing to say the least. To think of all the progress made, women who became leaders in their own right now being forced to withdraw once again from active public life, all that hard work that was put in by a well-meaning team perhaps being slowly undone.

But on a more hopeful note, I am optimistic that the institutions we built will outlive these uncertainties and eventually humanity will triumph.

Reaching out to isolated communities

Whatever it takes to reach the communities

Sometimes stranded by the weather or the availability of fuel

Braving roads covered by flooded rivers, sandstorms and snowstorms

Braving rickety bridges, flash-floods and checkpoints

Air transport of sorts

And more forms of transport

A rusty, leaking barge, circling B-52 bomber and a warning of unexploded ordnance are stark reminders of the risks involved

Emergency Food Distribution in Baghlan, Afghanistan

Emergency and permanent Water Supply in Baghlan, Mazar and Kabul

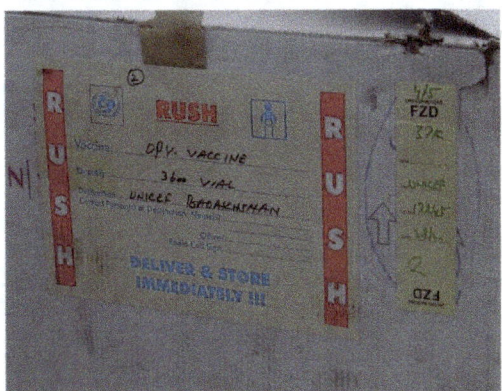

Routine vaccines for mothers and children. Cold Chain from Islamabad, Pakistan to villages in Afghan Badakshan.

Food for work initiatives in Afghan Badakshan

Transporting aid and distributing it to communities in and around the Buddha Caves of Bamiyan

Nutrition and education support for girls in Afghan Badakshan

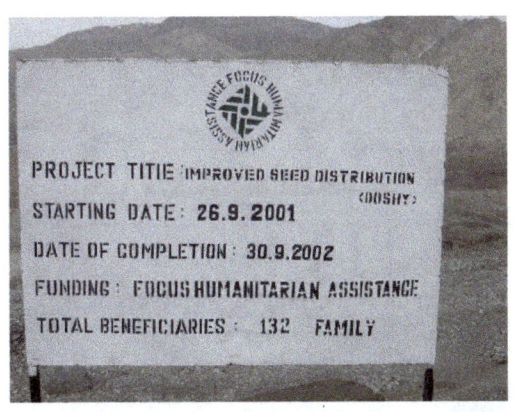

Support to farmers in Doshi, Baghlan

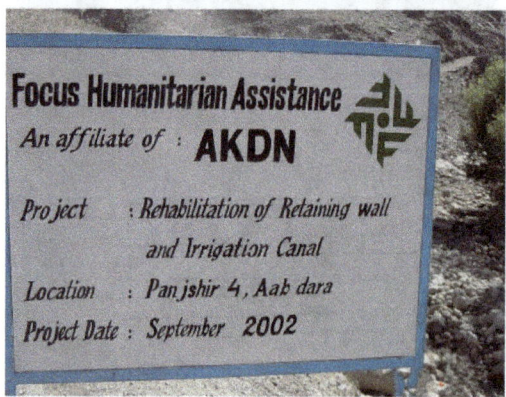

Partnerships and funding for rehabilitation projects

Before and after rehabilitation of a girls' school in Kabul

Before and after rehabilitation of a girls' school in Kabul

Rehabilitation: Girls back to university, children back to school, fields being irrigated

Faces of hope in town, rural and city

Chapter Two
Syria – Resilience In An Active War Zone

My engagement in Syria came in the wake of the civil war which broke out in early 2011 as an armed uprising against the regime of Syrian President Bashar al-Assad. I was the CEO of the Aga Khan Foundation (AKF) at the time, based in Russia – a very different landscape, to be covered further down this memoir.

The AKF CEO in Syria was a good friend of mine through our interactions during annual meetings in Switzerland or France over the years, contributing to much of my familiarity with this Eastern Mediterranean nation which I had yet to visit but would soon become deeply embedded in as the conflict escalated. As there was no FOCUS presence in Syria, the task of initiating the humanitarian response amid the civil war fell upon AKF. This being uncharted territory for the CEO at the time, we would often exchange ideas based on my first-hand experience of coordinating the response in a conflict and post-conflict setting in Afghanistan.

As his contract was coming to an end in early 2014 – the height of the civil war, my involvement became more active to ensure there isn't much of a gap between him leaving and the expansion of the humanitarian assistance work that was urgently required on the ground. I was given the charge of wrapping up in Russia – where I was stationed at the time – to get ready to take over the planning and execution of humanitarian work that would help build resilience amid a raging conflict in Syria. I set off on a preliminary visit to ensure a smooth transition and then quite quickly it was time to pack those bags and get right into the deep end.

Shift of Focus

The AKF presence in Salamiyah, western Syria, had been geared towards aspects such as agriculture to support farmers on a desert terrain, education, health and microfinance. The AKDN Syria Support Programme protocol with the government of Syria, which continues into the present day, meant that we also had a small presence in the capital Damascus.

Now, the development-led agenda of AKF had to be transformed into humanitarian assistance as the internally displaced persons (IDPs) and war-ravaged civilians were fighting for their day-to-day survival. The Food Aid programme had already been kick-started under the AKDN consolidated Syria Support Programme and once I got there, my remit was to start extending the humanitarian action.

Stepping into an active war zone, so far witnessed only in the form of harrowing images flashing across television screens or in newspapers, came with an obvious sense of trepidation of what lies ahead. The so-called Islamic State (ISIS) terrorist group had proved its sheer ruthlessness in the region time and time again – be it beheadings or bomb blasts – in pursuit of their own distorted version of "Islam", not one most fellow Muslims identified with.

Given this hawkish scenario, getting to Salamiyah itself proved a complex task. The only access we had was via Beirut, the capital of Lebanon. After an overnight stay in Beirut, it was a drive south along the Mediterranean through some breathtaking views to get to the Syrian city. The briefing from the outgoing CEO, who met us in Beirut, gave me a heads up on the live conflict zone that we were driving into. While the active fighting had reportedly not reached Salamiyah as yet, random suicide bombings and landing of rocket shells were not uncommon. This meant there was no way of knowing what was in store for us as we edged closer to the district.

Salamiyah stands at a geographical crossroad of this war-torn country – the mid-way point on the map south to north from Damascus to Aleppo and east to west from the ISIS stronghold of Raqqa to the Lebanon border. As a result, it was being heavily guarded by Russian-backed Syrian government forces to hold on to the very heart of the country from falling into ISIS hands.

Deathly Fireworks

The civil war had a two-pronged approach at the time, which involved ground forces combat as well as the prolific use of short-range ballistic missiles. Our journey to Salamiyah was taken up by briefings of how these missiles were being launched all over the place, including as a deterrent to any advancing forces. I did not want to get drawn too much into the war tactics of my new assignment, but it became apparent that the territory we were heading into would include deadly flying missiles as part of the daily routine.

At the border, there was no mistaking these ground realities as we were greeted with large hoardings of President Bashar Al-Assad as stark messaging to reiterate that he was still in charge here, and not ISIS. The process of immigration was another long-drawn one, with our passports handled in one building and the fees to be paid up for the entry visa in a separate building. This bureaucracy did little to calm the sense of apprehension I was already experiencing on being told the photocopier is out of action, extending our wait time at the border until some off-the-books Syrian Pound payments surreptitiously exchanged hands.

I had some sympathy for these local border force officials, surviving on very little by way of salary amid soaring inflation while undertaking life-threatening work, given that borders and checkpoints were always particularly vulnerable to a missile attack. However, our protocol with the Syrian government and diplomatic cards made most of this exchange quite friendly, or as friendly as a war zone can ever really feel. In fact, I will never forget the vision of a computer game like visual that presented itself as I looked out of the balcony of my apartment that was to become my home later in Salamiyah – the missiles and counter-missiles created a kind of deathly fireworks display that sent shivers down the spine. I soon learnt that not all the shots being fired were intended as an attack because reportedly the ISIS operatives also communicated with their forces on the ground by means of firing aerial shots. This air-borne coded messaging system resulted in incessant firing rounds reverberating throughout the day. In fact, over time, it was when things got too quiet that I felt rather uneasy with a sense of foreboding of what kind of an attack was being planned that would eventually break the uncharacteristic silence.

The sight of the bombarded landscape of what would once have been the bustling cities of Homs and Hama en route to Salamiyah are extremely distressing to this day, akin to the images of death and destruction in Gaza being beamed around the world during the conflict that began in October 2023. These Syrian cities had been razed to the ground and turned into ghost towns, with just stray dogs meandering the streets as any sign of life. The scraps of human clothing or a child's abandoned shoe stood out even more starkly in such a setting, raising disturbing thoughts and questions in the mind about the fate of that family – were they able to escape in time, or did a deadly missile take them by surprise?

As part of my familiarisation briefings, I had been given some basic instructions to learn to distinguish between the big bangs of the scores of missiles that were to become my daily companion. If the sound of the rocket launch is louder than the ensuing landing sound, it meant the trajectory is away from where I am at that point. However, if it's vice-versa and the landing sound is louder, it meant the missile was headed in my direction. Soon, I had my own first-hand experiences to fall back upon and became aware of a sharp whistle sound accompanying a missile making its way to land too close for comfort. However, being armed with this added knowledge of the trajectory of some of these death devices was of little use at the time as there was nothing to be done but sit tight and pray for the best. There were no bunkers or places of refuge to shelter in that could offer any lifesaving means following such an analysis.

The result was that news of fatalities soon became a harsh reality over the course of my stay there, including the tragic death of an aeronautical engineer I had come to know quite well. He had been just around 100 metres away from me when one of these missiles hit us. As a result, that death really hit me hard and jolts me to this day when I think back to that moment because I could just as easily have been the target and not survived to tell this tale. I can still feel the strong vibration from that particular missile attack back in 2017, with its shrapnel claiming many victims.

Another similar close shave with death was when we were driving in a bullet-proof vehicle and a missile was launched a few metres away which flew right over our car. The result was the vehicle being thrown up in the air sideways and fortunately landing back on the ground with a scary thud – quite the thrilling shot that would not have been out of place in an action-packed Hollywood blockbuster, but truly bone-chilling in real life. I dare not contemplate our fate had the car we were travelling in not been a bulletproof vehicle much heavier than a standard 4X4 drive.

Life Must Carry On

The mounting casualties from such attacks on the ground forces and those not lucky enough to have the protection of a bulletproof vehicle meant that my team were constantly having to expand the emergency capability of the Salamiyah District Hospital. We had our own back-up operational in the form of the Mass Casualty Management Centre to supplement the overflows from the Hospital.

Our mission essentially was to ensure that despite this deadly scenario, life must carry on to as much of a normal a degree as possible – for hospitals, schools and businesses to be able to function in some capacity. The humanitarian action, therefore, covered the basic amenities of food and water and psychosocial counselling for the IDPs moving into the centre of the district for protection as the conflict intensified in the outlying areas. This meant the population of Salamiyah increased three-fold, as judged by the local mayor based on the increased volumes of the refuse generated in the city.

After those early weeks of the initial orientation visit, I returned to take formal charge of my new posting in May 2014 and set about expanding the food programme for the growing number of IDPs. My own apartment block, made up of four homes, felt like a little safe haven ensconced within a volatile city – newly equipped with all the essentials. It was in a busy neighbourhood, walking distance from the main street in the very heart of the city, known as Hama Street. This also meant I was close to where the Karamani Ismaili Jamatkhana was located, fostering a very strong sense of community with regular interactions over daily prayers. In fact, my presence as a senior representative of AKF sent to care for the Jamat and those who lived among them seemed to add a further dimension of welfare amid the war zone.

It later emerged that every time I had to leave the city – for a tour of Damascus, Tartous or Khawabi, a meeting in Geneva, or even a short home visit to my family in London – there was some unease within the Jamat about my absence. The close-knit community wondered if it was an indication of a looming attack that the senior representative of AKF had been evacuated from Salamiyah. So, I made it a point to update the *Mukhi* (chief) any time I had to undertake an official or private visit outside of the city during my four-year posting in Syria to reassure the community.

Soon, the district was to become a reasonable safe zone for all communities – not just Ismailis – as people fled their homes, sometimes temporarily to escape ISIS attacks but often permanently. As we were in a strategically important location, the government enforced tougher ring-fencing but, of course, the threat of insurgencies always loomed large.

The immediate focus was on distributing the food and non-food aid, in collaboration with the World Food Programme (WFP), to the families in need and my notes indicate that as many as 10,000 food baskets were handed out to over 50,000 beneficiaries on a monthly basis. The quota of rations of household essentials for each local host family was calculated based on the IDPs they were sheltering. Many families had selflessly offered refuge to those displaced from their homes as the civil war raged on.

Water Sanitation and Hygiene, referred to as WASH for short, was the next big priority for the team, with hundreds of water storage tanks of varying sizes to be installed in schools, medical and community centres and water deficit neighbourhoods. This work was carried out in conjunction with the Ministry of Education and the local Mayor, based on our established model of collaborating with the locals to identify their needs and priorities for the community. Water is an absolute essential for life and this provision was combined with the concept of hygiene and sanitation. This involved additional female toilets being installed based on the requirement and in schools, teachers included aspects such as the importance of hand washing in the curriculum.

Meanwhile, in the health category, there was an important partnership with the World Health Organisation (WHO) and United Nations International Children's Emergency Fund (UNICEF) for a polio immunisation campaign. Our outreach volunteer teams followed up to ensure any children not covered under the organisations' routine immunisation drive received the life-saving drops in time. Other steps included the provision of supplementary nutritional feeds for babies as part of the WFP's Plumpy'Doz initiative. These distribution points created as temporary hubs or within local schools doubled up as awareness centres for parents, enforcing an integrated approach with different strands of our health initiatives working effectively in tandem.

Over time, we had a permanent space for the food distribution, complete with a waiting room and toilets, soon to be replicated by other agencies impressed with its smooth functioning and multi-dimensional approach.

Lasting Impact

While ongoing battles and skirmishes were a harsh reality, there were other more uplifting facets to my Syrian assignment. Overlooking the balcony of my apartment was a large empty space, effectively an abandoned dirt patch. One evocative memory is watching this discarded piece of land come to life right before my eyes as I actioned AKDN's Programme for Social Spaces. It was born out of an instinct as I watched young children being abruptly dispersed by large vehicles rolling in to disrupt their innocent game of marbles on that patch – just like the game I played as a little boy in Kenya. After discussions with the neighbours and the Mayor, we settled upon the idea of turning this little field into a children's playground and a park for the wider community. Soon, this took the form of a wider programme as dirt patches dotted all over the city began being similarly transformed.

Over the years, I recall looking out from my balcony and feeling a powerful sense of gratification watching children playing on the swings and slides that were installed in the park or even just doing their homework under the solar lighting that was eventually rolled out. It became a hangout for all age groups, as they gathered around the benches over several cups of *mate* tea – a local staple, made of dried leaves of the plant known as Yerba Mate.

I could see the impact of our Social Spaces model unfold right before my eyes – it engendered dialogue and social cohesion as people converged upon this leafy space equipped with solar power, especially during the inevitable power cuts in the battle-weary city. The model was designed to showcase that no matter your background or faith, these social spaces were a hub for all and that there was strength in diversity and pluralism. As this hub of activity grew in size and popularity, with people heading to this preferred meeting point daily in shifts as and when they wrapped up work, it also helped small self-employed businesses to flourish. Popcorn and candy vendors sprang up spotting a demand among the groups socialising on holidays or simply at the end of a hard day's shift. Shops and small cafés soon dotted all seven such Social Spaces our organisation helped established during that phase.

Food, water and shelter were the topmost priorities in the war-torn region, but such initiatives were equally crucial to help with the long-term psychosocial wellbeing of the community. Syria, a middle-income country with a well-educated population, may not have been very well developed but it wasn't poverty-stricken either. Against this backdrop, my priorities were also to ensure the schools, hospitals and clinics carried on operating as smoothly as possible. The AKDN

Microfinance Bank was providing women-headed households with finance for their initiatives, and it was important this work carried on unencumbered despite the civil war. The most important aspect of my assignment was to ensure that humanitarian action and recovery went hand in hand.

With that in mind, one of the key initiatives was the Community Emergency Response Team (CERT). Six CERTs of 10 volunteers each – men and women aged between their 20s and 40s – were already mobilised by the time I took charge and four more were added on to create 10 teams in all. These CERTs were deployed for the needs of the Salamiyah district and the villages of Sabboura and Al Kasson. The unpaid volunteers were taken to Beirut for their Mass Casualty Management (MCM) training by our trainers, who in turn were trained by Rapid UK (later RedR). They would be provided with certificates and the required gear and return to Salamiyah fully equipped to intervene in any mass casualty situation, be it bombings or missile attacks. They were trained in basic first response to evacuate people from dangerous buildings, coordinate fire rescue and provide emergency intervention before the ambulances arrived to move patients to the hospital.

One of my early tasks was to source a CT scanner for the Salamiyah Hospital and also oversee its expansion, with its emergency department under immense pressure to enhance its operating capacity from four to seven rooms as the war took its toll and the trolleys of injured civilians rolled in. This expansion covered not just bed space but required essential provisions of oxygen tanks and other life-saving equipment. After an initial assessment, our team had installed an additional Trauma Centre to act as a buffer in the event of mass casualties as a triage unit. Of the four ambulances donated for our cause, two were deployed to the Salamiyah Hospital and the other two ear-marked for use by the new Trauma Centre.

Long-Term View

It was with a long-term view, looking beyond the war, that I was tasked to execute AKDN's Multi-Input Programme for the region to cover the full spectrum of humanitarian, recovery and rehabilitation interventions.

Our vocational training centres, known as Continuing Education Workshop Centres (CEWCs), offered courses to equip the local population with the very basic reconstruction skills that would be required in rebuilding the nation. Courses such as office management, English language lessons, household electrical repair, air conditioning system maintenance, hairdressing, tailoring, business management, solar power expertise and elderly care were all designed to enhance the future employability of the trainees who signed up. The idea was to equip both men and women with some essential skills that would stand them in good stead and hundreds signed up to access this training over time.

With the help of professional partners, it replicated a successful programme from Damascus that was retrofitted to the context of Salamiyah. On graduation, these newly trained professionals were handed certificates and a comprehensive toolkit to put their training into action. The very first cohort of women got together to start their own small electrical wiring business with the help of a loan from AKDN's Microfinance Bank – Aga Khan Agency for Microfinance (AKAM). It also meant that some of the women-headed households in the city now had the comfort of employing women for their electrical needs. It proved to be one of the most successful programmes, like our Social Spaces initiative, and was personally heart-warming for me to observe women get trained in skills that may have traditionally been viewed as a male domain.

The objectives were manifold – not only to impart critical skills but also to get the youth off the streets and away from radicalising forces. There were set criteria to attract unemployed youth and a very minimal fee imposed to ensure the course was taken seriously and not dismissed as being a free handout. The contrast that emerged was stark – while some youngsters were inevitably lured by the militia, a majority chose a different route and committed to making their lives better with dedication. The thousands of volunteers who joined us were shining examples, with young men and women selflessly training in Mass Casualty Management to help those wounded by the frequent missiles being fired all over the place.

Another important initiative was the setting up of nine Early Learning Centres for the children of the IDPs, aged between three and six years, to provide them with a safe space where they could learn and also get some help to cope with the trauma of war. These centres were set up in the Jamatkhanas but were open to all communities in two shifts to accommodate all the children, who were managed by well trained teachers employed by our organisation. Post-traumatic stress disorder (PTSD) in conflict zones where bombs and missiles are a daily reality is of great concern and such interventions were crucial for young children. One of the other focus areas was to train government health workers on psychosocial support for young children to help them prevent and overcome PTSD. They would then oversee summer clubs and open days for children aged four to 15 to have a fun day out, be it with games, face painting or other activities. These often took the form of massive street parties utilising the Social Spaces for the children. It was heartening to see children and adults being able to set aside the harsh realities of being displaced by war at least for some time.

One instance has been etched in mind from this time when during one such open day activity, children were asked to paint what they dreamt of the previous night. The resulting paintings haunt me to this day with their mostly black and dark hues – tanks, fighter planes and machine guns among the images these young children's dreams were being invaded by. The second part of the activity was for them to paint over these to create images of what they would like to dream about. These brightly hued creations would bring tears to anyone's eyes – an overbearing tank would get transformed into a colourful cosy home with a playground where children were frolicking around, and a frightening fighter jet would get transformed into a more docile passenger plane. This alteration of what these young children were visualising every night to what they would like to dream about is reflective of what we all aspire to in life – portrayed with childlike innocence but nonetheless making a profound point against war and in favour of peace.

This innocuous little exercise was visibly fulfilling the objective of helping these children overcome their trauma as they craved to leave the darkness behind and embrace all the colours that life has to offer. I did get a strong sense that the activity was helping these children, in whatever small way, as we went village to village and neighbourhood to neighbourhood with this initiative. This coincided with the distribution of essential school supplies, including chalk, paper, stationery and refurbished desks to expand the capacity of local schools as they accommodated the ever-increasing number of pupils from the IDPs moving into Salamiyah.

For their parents, there was support for farmers in the form of seeds and fertilisers and support for women-headed households to set up their cottage industries. So, the idea was an integrated response in order to address immediate humanitarian needs, security, water, maternal and child health, education and economic livelihood. In partnership with international organisations, AKDN staff and volunteers dedicated their efforts to provide humanitarian assistance to over 30,000 vulnerable families in Salamiyah district, many of whom were IDPs.

The district suffered from increasing water deficit for over 60 years, which only became more challenging as the crisis intensified. Less than 4 per cent of Salamiyah residents had access to the recommended minimum amount of water. A shortage of power meant many families were forced to spend their limited income on water and diesel. One of AKDN's priorities, therefore, was to assist the families to meet basic water needs by installing community managed water storage tanks.

The natural water source to Salamiyah from the Euphrates River had been occupied by ISIS and with the constant threat of missiles to alternate sources of water supplies, I identified the importance of ensuring an enduring solution to this very basic need of the households. It was obvious that trucking in water through other cities, which had to be fully tested and purified, was not an ideal long-term solution. Salamiyah did have access to water, but it was buried deep underground and hence the answer was to partner with the government to dig wells to reach that natural water source. AKDN went on to set up a Reverse Osmosis Plant worth $1.6 million as a turnkey operation to provide a reliable water source to the city and nearby areas.

To provide a more durable response to the political and security situation, we established local water treatment and distribution facilities to ensure long-lasting drinking water supply. Therefore, investments in building capacities, sustaining the spirit of volunteerism and engagement of communities represented the main pillars of AKDN's work in Syria at the time. These pillars contributed to building resilience, anchoring communities, accelerating recovery and building hope for a brighter future.

Looking back to my time in conflict-torn Syria, I recall some very palpable outcomes of AKDN's work in support of all communities. Seeing children going to school or engaging with the Early Learning Centres was a very heart-warming feeling indeed. All the background intensive work that went into getting many of these initiatives up and running paid off in spades when I could see the impact on the ground. For instance, there was a distinct divide between life after the solar panels we were able to install and the time before. They quite literally lit up the very heart of the community, with the days of noisy generators during congregational prayers a thing of the past. The solar-powered community centres were open 24/7 for children to use for their exam revision and I can never forget the sheer dedication shown by young students during exam prep, well aware that in education lay their future prospects.

As the CEO of the operation in Syria, the buck stopped with me. Not only did the responsibility of the 400 staff on our payroll and around 1,000 volunteers spread across the areas covered by our initiatives, but also the future hopes and aspirations of the community under my charge weighed heavily on me day in and day out. The security situation was also never far from the mind, even as I travelled around daily to conduct site visits. It was an intensive phase that my body chemistry somehow never seemed to adjust to because it never allowed me rest on the official day off, which fell on a Friday. As a result, on Sundays it felt strange to be working through like a usual working day.

Meanwhile, several dangerous situations unfolded without any notice. I recall an instance when ISIS attacked a village just 20 miles away forcing the women and children to flee towards Salamiyah for protection. Obviously, it meant all the routine work had to be paused to make suitable arrangements for the influx of these traumatised families – from mattresses and blankets to basic food aid. Alongside, there was the urgent need to update WFP to supplement our depleted provisions due to the additional emergency requirements. We also had our own security protocols in the event of such attacks, ensuring timely lockdowns and communicating with officials out in the field through radios in their cars to caution them to rush to safety in the face of an imminent threat.

We also had contingency plans for mass evacuations in place for every scenario because if ISIS was to breach the security perimeter of Salamiyah, the recriminations would have been bloody. This involved extremely complex and confidential planning, balancing several aspects even as the day-to-day work carried on in parallel. The first few years were the toughest, in terms of the conflict and also to get the programmes up and running in an active war zone. By 2016-17, when I had been there for over two years, the systems felt well entrenched and all the programmes we had initiated were operating rather smoothly. The foundations were firmly set, and all this was achieved against the backdrop of some very challenging geopolitics at play.

When I reflect on my time in Syria during that phase, provision of the basic survival needs, the social spaces that engendered peace and community cohesion, the Early Childhood Education initiatives, the permanent water supply solutions in case of emergency or drought, the support to farmers to restart or increase production, and the longer-term vocational training stand out in my mind. As the world's attention gets diverted to several other unfolding crises around the world, I can take heart in the enduring legacy of some of AKDN's programmes that were designed to provide a base for the future generations to build upon and to keep the region's economy going under dire circumstances.

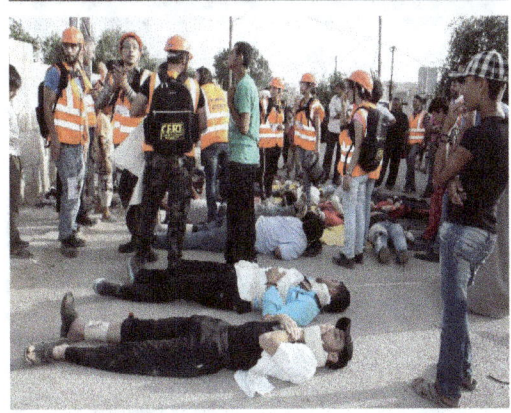
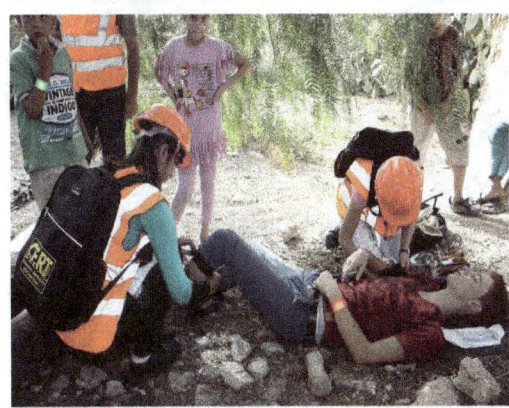

Community Emergency Response Team (CERT) training in search & rescue, triage, stabilise

Food aid: Assessment, storage and distribution

Food aid beneficiaries: Taking home their monthly ration

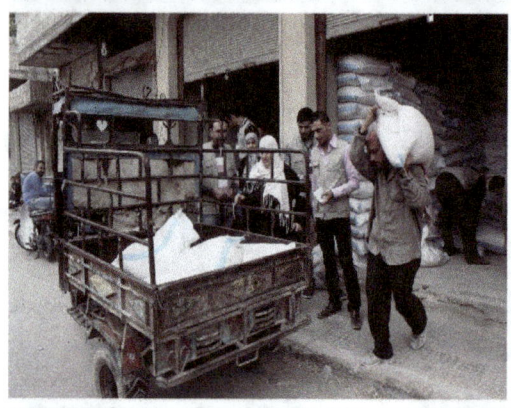

Livelihood support to farmers: Need assessment and distribution of improved seeds

Water supply: Emergency, temporary and permanent

Psychosocial support: Volunteer-led street parties and open days for children

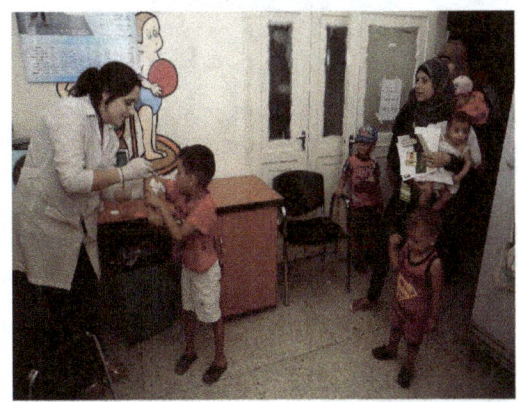

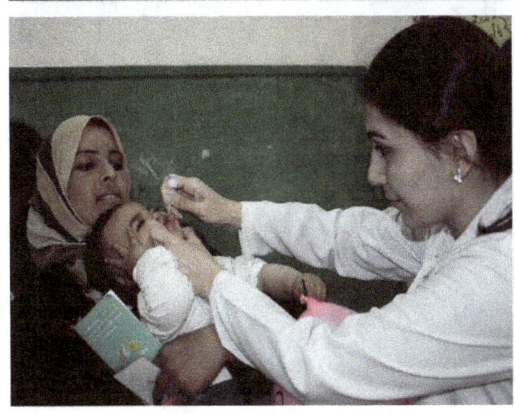

Emergency health: Routine immunization and nutrition support for children

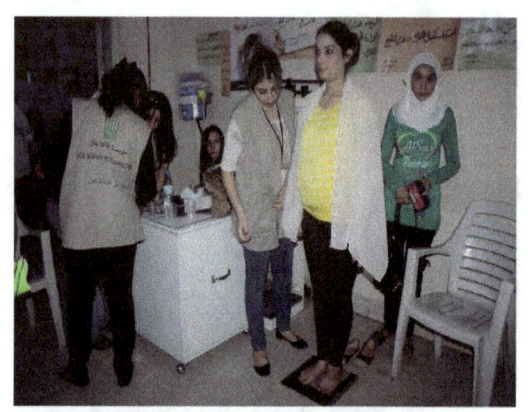

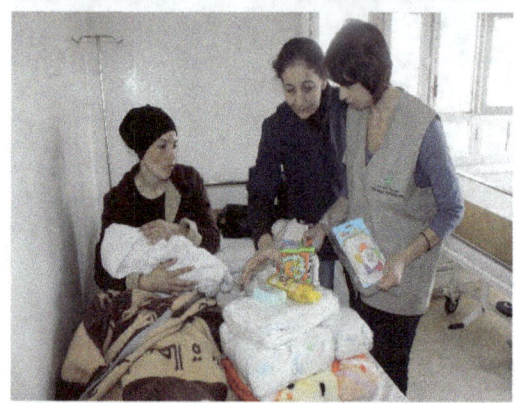

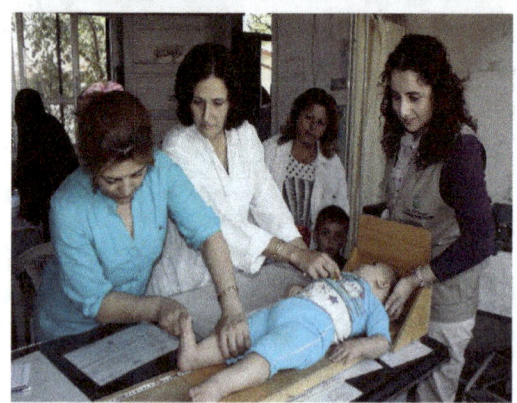

Mother & Child Health (MCH): prenatal, newborn and infant

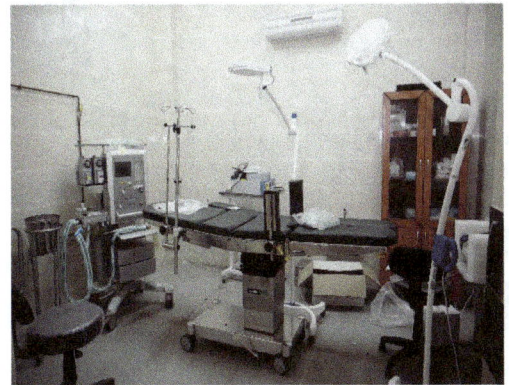

*Health capacity building:
Clinics, accident & emergency and hospital*

Early Childhood Development (ECD)
early learning centres and parental support

*Community cohesion:
Solar-lit, safe social spaces to gather, meet and play*

Financial support for vulnerable families, augment emergency call-out and train trainers

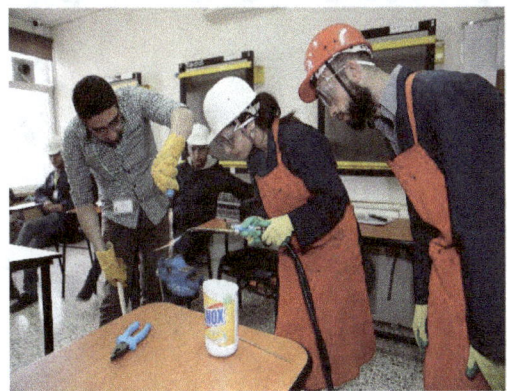

Vocational Training: AC repair, electric appliance repair and hair dressing courses, most subscribed to

Faces of hope

Chapter Three
Russia – An Expedition Breaking New Ground

After my tenure in Afghanistan, I returned to the UK where my connection with the region continued through organising training sessions and crisis management planning as part of the International Disaster Response brief between 2003 and 2007.

This was to be followed by my next major assignment – as Head of the Representative Office of the Aga Khan Foundation (AKF), Geneva, in other words as the CEO in charge of set-up and operations in Russia. Since the collapse of the Soviet Union in 1992, there had been an influx of labour migrants into Russia from former Soviet states such as Tajikistan – which suffered the double whammy of a termination of support from the motherland coupled with a lack of arable land and having to flee a raging civil war.

While these migrants were largely absorbed into the informal economy as workers across sectors such as construction, hospitality and domestic work, there was a growing need within these displaced communities for a helping hand. This was the gap the AKF wanted to address by better organising these diasporas to create lasting support networks for healthcare and education provisions, through

Early Childhood Development (ECD) initiatives, tutorials for school-aged children and youth camps. These were coordinated with the help of capacity building of staff, volunteers and diaspora-led formal and informal units, with a view to support the establishment of formal civil society institutions.

What lay ahead of me was a very different kind of challenge, not a war or disaster zone but a country slowly emerging from behind the cloak of Communism – a scenario unlike any other I had ever encountered. The laws and regulations in Russia of the early 2000s were very much a legacy of the Soviet era, with the Cold War still casting a long shadow over the workings of the bureaucracy.

As this role was a brand-new position, my posting got the required sign off from AKDN Committee (Head Office) and then off went the paperwork for the Russian authorities to assess the application for my role as Head of AKF's Representative Office in the country, with a brief to assist disadvantaged migrant groups. Ours was just one among multiple international organisations setting up their operations in post-Cold-War Russia, which resulted in a mountainous pile of documentation on the in-tray of the authorities to review and process. So, by the time my clearance papers came through the various channels in that long queue, I had been waiting 18 months even as I prepared the groundwork. There was an added dimension to my usual pre-posting prep work as the relocation to Moscow was to be family posting, as opposed to a solo mission.

My wife D'jemilla and I decided that our youngest son would be joining us on this posting because our older son and daughter had their own job and university obligations at the time. It was in July 2007 that I first set off on my own to find an apartment in Moscow before my son could begin his school term in a few months' time and that was to be the start of our seven-year expedition in Russia as a family.

Stark Contrasts

The image of Russia planted in my mind was from my very first visit back in 1995 as part of the advance team for His Highness' tour. But what I encountered on landing in Moscow more than a decade later was a entirely transformed country, starting with a much-upgraded modernised airport. One of the most striking contrasts from that former visit hit me as I stepped out on to the street – it was foreign car brands such as Mercedes and Toyota that dominated the roads, replacing the majority Russian-made models like Lada and Volga of the past. What I encountered was a very palpable shift from the rather dark and dingy 1990s to a bright and shiny modern-day post-Soviet Russian capital.

My office in those early days before we shifted to larger, more permanent premises was located in a very sophisticated Moscow

Academy of Sciences building, amid a cluster of famous iconic buildings dating back to the Stalinist era in the heart of the city known as the Seven Sisters. This symbol of Soviet Russia now stood cheek by jowl with the new glass-fronted high-rises that had come up in the past few years.

However, I soon discovered that while on the surface much seemed different, the Soviet systems of the past were still very deeply entrenched and apparent every step of the way. I recall my sense of bemusement when the same unsmiling guard at the Academy of Sciences who had been waiving me through after cursorily checking my ID card suddenly pointed out that my card had now expired and refused me entry to my office. He knew exactly what I did and which office I belonged to and visited daily, but he was bound by the inflexibility of a bureaucratic system that was ingrained in their psyche, which prevented them from even considering a more pragmatic or flexible approach. I couldn't help but note that their uniforms also added to this uncompromising veneer, which had perhaps hardened over the course of a rather rigid Soviet upbringing that trained them never to let their guard down. I did wonder whether as Westerners our outgoing and cheery demeanour made them uneasy because that's just not how they did things in this country.

Such social anomalies were compounded by an alien language to make my first few months in Moscow quite trying. It was some time before we had a professor from the Moscow State University come home to coach me and my wife in the Russian language, which made life much easier as we went about our day-to-day chores or to buy groceries at the local supermarket. The more I learnt to read and write Russian, which I am quite well-versed in even today, I discovered how this rich language has a lot of words that can be traced back to Sanskrit. D'jemilla was always better at the written word and my skill lay in conversational Russia, which meant over time we were quite the double act as a team in this alien land.

Getting Started

I kick-started my work in Russia with an initial assessment process to establish the needs of the community we were there to serve and to navigate the local laws and legal framework as a new Representative Office of an international organisation.

I discovered that there were several students from Tajikistan who had come to Russia on AKF scholarships to study medicine. Through my contact with one such medical student from Kenya, one of my first initiatives was to create a network of doctors under the umbrella of the Ismaili Doctors' Initiative (IDI). Through a central hotline managed by a staff member, anybody within the Tajik diaspora network in Russia who required medical assistance would be able to access this service at no cost. Our analysis estimated a diaspora of around 25,000 to 30,000 that was spread across different cities, with the largest cluster of around 18,000 located in Moscow, followed by smaller clusters in Yekaterinburg, St. Petersburg, Samara and Gagarin – named after the Soviet cosmonaut, Yuri Gagarin, the first man to land in space. I would regularly travel to these regions, some accessible by car from Moscow but others like Yekaterinburg necessitating a flight and for St. Petersburg, the cultural hub of the country, a four-hour express or an overnight route by train was one of the most pleasant tours on my regular schedule.

There are many laudable aspects to Russian policies, including a highly efficient transport system and a health system that is free at the point of delivery. However, because a number of migrants were living undocumented in the country, they were wary of accessing the state-funded medical services. This is where the IDI network stepped in to offer crucial assistance to the migrant labourers by handholding them through the processes. We facilitated this by supporting the doctors to be able to volunteer their services and by the time I left Russia there were around 30 doctors enrolled on to the IDI, supporting hundreds of people in need. We also provided transport and logistics for these doctors and nurses to visit construction sites where the migrant labourers were employed to make presentations, disseminate life-saving public health messages, and undertake important medical checks on site.

Many of these workers had survived extremely harsh conditions as they made their passage to Russia in over-crowded containers. Their overriding objective was to be able to earn enough wages to survive, support their loved ones and save a little to send money back home to their families still in Tajikistan. Looking after their health was not a priority and having the IDI volunteers undertake on-site visits made a huge difference to their lives. My contacts in the region inform me that the referrals they get through this system has multiplied over the years and they continue to use messaging systems to disseminate health information to expectant mothers around life-saving immunisation and alerts for those at risk from common conditions such as hypertension and diabetes. As an extension of this health programme, we were able to incorporate home visits and a more regularised system of construction site visits over time.

Finding Our Feet

Soon it was time to move out of the constraints of the Academy of Sciences premises into a more expansive two-hall open plan establishment in a large entertainment centre, complete with a roller blading rink and restaurants. The Tajik migrant beneficiaries of our services were visibly more comfortable within these friendlier environs than the guarded-up constraints of a Soveit-era academy. As a result, this new central venue served our multi-purpose needs of a well-equipped open plan office space and an ideal site for the various family-oriented programmes we had mapped out for the community.

The starting point was with the Early Childhood Development (ECD), designed to support families through the needs of their children aged zero to eight years old. ECD covers a series of components and modules, including the First Steps Programme which is geared towards newborns to three-year-olds. Our ECD programme underwent a series of phases as the scope and local membership expanded over the course of weeks and months.

Based on well-documented research, the early years in a child's life are crucial to their healthy long-term development and therefore we had some tried and tested modules from our work around the globe that could now be tailored for the needs of these children living in Russia. The ECD programme is designed based on neuroscientific research which shows that the brain of a child develops the most from birth to ages two, three, four and five and therefore it is important to have the right kind of educational engagement with this age range. In line with this thinking, we also had a Reading For Children programme tied in, which was targeted at all age groups including the parents who struggled with their Russian language lessons.

My wife, being a qualified early-years practitioner, was the volunteer heading up these initiatives – from designing the modules to organising the training for the local teachers through qualified

Russian tutors. Over a period of time, we kick-started a Tutorial Assistance Programme for primary schoolchildren who may find themselves lagging behind in class before they can progress to the secondary level. All these drives were interconnected in one way or another, with annual residential Youth Camps in the summer also incorporating some of the learnings from the other initiatives. The AKF Scholarship Invitations, aimed at post-graduate students, were available for students as an independent education initiative.

Beyond the education system, we had a Psychosocial Support Programme run through confidential telephone counselling and manned by professional counsellors who addressed the mental health concerns of the community, intensified by the anxieties of migration and challenging work-life circumstances. The Civil Society Sector initiatives included a Small Grants Programme and Capacity Building Programme. These were aimed at supporting local community leaders with funds and mentorship to set up their own civil society efforts, such as running a non-governmental organisation (NGO).

They were trained in managing these units with the help of community volunteers, who were then well equipped to implement their own initiatives. Their efforts included organising cultural music and dance events to keep the traditions of the country of their origin alive in Russia. These groups also coordinated and managed a pool of communal funds to finance the medical needs of the contributors and would also step in during a crisis, such as the repatriation of the deceased back home to their villages in Tajikistan for the funeral.

Parvis Bhatia, a qualified English teacher volunteer from Canada with experience of teaching the language in Tajikistan and Afghanistan, was enrolled as part of the capacity building initiatives we undertook in Moscow. These English classes extended to the doctors who were part of the IDI service and one of the volunteers, Dr Khimat – who hardly spoke a word of English when he started – attributes a large part of his later successes to these lessons. He went on to head the Aga Khan Health Service in Tajikistan for a few years and to this day credits these classes for helping him better communicate in his line of work.

To manage these different yet interconnected strands of our work, we had the Health Coordinator, Education Coordinator and Civil Society Coordinator working alongside staffers in charge of finance, legal, and logistics requirements of the Moscow office. The workers included local Russians and some of Tajik heritage, who offered the beneficiaries the comfort level of being able to communicate in their own language too.

Working Within Parameters

In those early days of my new Russian assignment, I had a natural urge to pack in a lot across these different spheres – be it health, education, or economic upliftment. But the reality was that we were bound by certain constraints as a Representative Office, with very limited set of initiatives permitted within that remit.

Fortunately, by virtue of AKDN's wide network, we had the services of two of the biggest international legal firms at our disposal on a pro bono basis. I found myself constantly having to bounce off my ambitious plans with them to check how far I could scale up an operation I had mapped out for launch. Of course, I was determined to stay within the framework of the local laws and this rather tedious approach was therefore unavoidable. Nevertheless, I tried to push the envelope as much as possible to upgrade the scope of our work as far as was legally permissible.

There were the added requirements of reporting to the Russian Ministry of Justice every six months and presenting an annual report on the nature of activities we were undertaking, with the corresponding expenditure. I ensured this was done diligently and submitted in time. It meant a whole lot of admin work, with a load of contracts to be drafted for the local service providers we had hired. There were several layers of compliance paperwork involved to back up our operations as a new Representative Office in a country yet to emerge fully from its Soviet-era legacy.

I was keenly aware that I was operating in a territory with its own set of unfamiliar rules and often found myself having to scale back some plans to the point that was deemed "safe" within the legal framework. I did stretch most of our development initiatives to the maximum, but I still have the sense that there was certainly more that could have been achieved if we weren't operating within such strict parameters.

With the help of a local NGO, the diaspora community already had a Sunday initiative going, as part of which they would rent a hall and hold sessions on Moral and Ethical Studies for six- to 16-year-olds. And, while these classes took place, the parents of these children participated in talks and presentations organised on faith and other topics that would prove useful to them as migrants, such as advice on local laws, citizenship advisory, making a will and important health messaging. These groups would make the trek from far and wide as a family for these weekly gatherings. What our team observed was that while these classes took place, the youngest children aged between three to six were at a loose end while their parents and older siblings were engaged in their respective activities. This offered an important window of opportunity with a captive audience at hand for us to piggyback on this ongoing programme to facilitate our ECD modules for early childhood development. As the hall was already being hired, we were provided some space within that set up for our classrooms for three- to six-year-olds centred around a play-and-learn model.

Based on ECD Science, the focus was on designing activities and workshops that would initiate neuron connections in the brain for these young developing minds that happens mostly through play. The aim was to simultaneously enable the right kind of home environment for them to help enhance their brain development. There were various low-cost, no-cost activities and toys geared towards this goal. As an example, instead of offering children a jigsaw puzzle that would conclude with the same result each time, we would opt for building blocks that not only promoted hand-eye coordination but also resulted in new shapes and creations each time. Hence the model we followed was simple yet effective in encouraging brain connections through innovative playing techniques.

I also recall a Dressing Up Corner emerging during these sessions, which would have costumes for the children to play with. They had the chance to role play as a nurse or a doctor or a police officer, which subtly imparted ambitious and healthy social messaging far removed from any toys such as guns that engender thoughts of aggression in the young minds. Similarly, the Reading Corner promoted another healthy habit, and an Arts & Crafts Corner encouraged them to try their hand at creating objects through cut and paste. The dolls they played with also came subtly wrapped up in positive inclusivity messaging, encompassing figurines of all shapes, sizes and colours.

One activity that the children really enjoyed which has stayed with me till date was called "float and sink" – it involved a simple bowl of water and any household item, be it a coin or a bottle cap or any other handy object lying around. This object would be dropped into the bowl of water to see if sinks or floats. And the Eureka! moment that would flash in the eyes of these little children with this simple law of physics in action was a vision to behold. It is an example of a low-cost fun exercise that was inadvertently teaching these young minds about the Archimedes Principle and preparing them for their school years ahead in a creative and light-hearted way.

Meanwhile, their parents were learning more about creating a similar learning friendly environment at home, making use of objects such as a newspaper to get little children involved in engaging activities. It also became a great family bonding exercise, especially over the freezing months when many of them were homebound due to heavy snowfalls. We started our programme with a group of around 30-40 which kept growing over time into hundreds and soon required bigger halls and eventually different shifts to accommodate them all.

There was a very visible impact unfolding right before our eyes, which was extremely heartening for both me and my wife, whose programme designed for children is running to this day. Official statistics also reveal that children who underwent an ECD module had higher retention in school later and it would not be a stretch to say that it had a positive impact on their grades over time. The parents appreciated the benefits of these activities, which also nurtured friendships between different groups and had the added impact of community cohesion.

Soon, we spotted a need to expand our programme targeted at newborns to ensure the parents were aware of their rights and also had some basic assistance in caring for their babies – from immunisation to early brain development. The first step was to produce a Newborn Kit, which included all such basic health information with some additional inputs such as the child's very first cloth book and toy. This was followed up with training sessions on childproofing homes and other essential newborn care advice, as a booster to the free state-funded healthcare. Making a case for funding this programme proved very easy, and it went on to be a big success within just a few months' time.

> Research has demonstrated the many benefits of parents reading with their children from an early age. Being read to is one of the strongest predictors of academic success. Reading for Children is a simple yet powerful concept, designed in order to meet the needs of children and families who otherwise may have little or no opportunity to engage in reading.
>
> (Source: AKDN)

In parallel, we had launched the Reading For Children initiative which had been well-researched and tried and tested by AKDN in Kyrgyzstan – where it proved very popular and even won an award from the Shell Foundation. Under this scheme, trainers would train other facilitators who in turn would train parents on how to read along with their child and select age-appropriate books. This was based on scientific analysis that such an exercise enhanced the bond between children and their parents, retention in school, encouraged an interest in learning and made the children "classroom ready".

The module was created in a way that helped children grasp the concept of colours and counting, with an element of inquiry built in to make things interactive for the child, who is prompted to ask questions. The Kyrgyzstan model was designed with its nomadic communities in mind, for the families to carry these libraries of books as they travelled. It was soon incorporated into the state curriculum and AKDN decided to replicate this success story in other parts of the world.

It was an easy programme to incorporate because these books could be passed on from generation to generation as a circular library. In Russia, we noticed a wider benefit that grandparents with sketchy Russian were learning along with their grandchildren through this Reading For Children initiative. So, with benefits multi-pronged in most households, our library soon became quite a hive of activity for the families who could see the immense positive impact of the initiative.

Life as Expatriates

On a personal level, all this took place against the backdrop of getting used to a very different kind of lifestyle in Moscow where everyone lived in apartments that benefitted from state-funded heating. Around September-October, when the temperatures dropped to a consistently low Celsius, the heating system of the apartment blocks would automatically kick in. Every home, every office, every school and establishment was well heated and cosy regardless of the economic or immigration status of the inhabitants. Come April-May, when the temperatures rose to a certain high, the heating would automatically cut out.

The efficiency of the local council also comes to mind here, with heavy snow being cleared constantly and gritters at work non-stop during the harsh winter months. Life simply carried on as normal even as the snow continued to pile high, with de-icers being applied to the wings of aircraft to ensure smooth air traffic as well. Quite the contrast to even some modern-day cities in UK and Europe, where life can come to a standstill following even one or two days of snowfall.

Over time, as the novelty wore off, the harsh Moscow winters certainly did get monotonous. After a few Christmas holidays of quality family time and ski trips, our children had enough of this uniquely Russian white Christmas experience. The festive period also falls later in the year in Russia, which means from New Year's Day to January 10th everything completely shuts down for the holidays. Most Muscovites head out to their country homes or *dachas*, which are also popular as their weekend retreats.

Our early days were packed with a series of unusual experiences, including the process of learning how to drive on the other side of the road than Britain. On the subject of driving, there were further tricky matters to navigate such as the difficulty of acquiring a company car without giving in to the accepted norm of greasing the palms of the local number plate licensing authorities. I recall having to make several visits to the same office with the official in charge raising dubious issues with the translation on the bilingual form, filled out in English by me and translated by my driver on the corresponding side in Russian. The demand for an exact translation of certain words and phrases was an impossible ask because of the way sentences are constructed in the two languages.

Soon it was obvious the objections were merely a ruse to break my resolve that our organisation would not be associated with handing out any bribes. This resolve had hardened after a long-drawn wait for a bank account to be created in the name of the AKF Representative Office. On day three of unreasonable encounters at the driving licence office, I went in with my laptop and every time the official came up with a new objection, I would make the change instantly and re-submit the form there and then. Eventually, I wore him down because he realised he was fighting a losing battle for a bribe with me! The locals there were accustomed to carrying a few hundred Russian Roubles in their pockets for such eventualities, with the police and other low-paid officials notoriously corrupt. Be that as it may, I was determined that an AKF rep would not be coerced into this casual bribery.

These day-to-day matters proved quite tedious but having a diplomatic card at hand certainly eased our way around things somewhat. On the rare occasions that I was stopped by traffic cops, that ID card often sufficed. One such cop, clearly on the lookout for a few quick Roubles, stopped me at a junction to ask exactly how inebriated I was, to which I calmly replied in my limited Russian *tol'ko chay* (only tea). He cracked up at this phrase and enjoyed a good laugh with his colleague before waiving me through, realising quite wisely that I wasn't worth pursuing for any bribes.

My interaction with the Bank of Moscow stands out as a very pleasant experience amidst a series of less-friendly bureaucratic exchanges, where they not only welcomed the prospect of having our organisation bank with them but also upgraded us as a premium customer. They appreciated the community work AKF was undertaking and wanted to be seen to support that as part of their corporate social responsibility. This was after a series of banks had outright rejected our business on rather flimsy grounds.

Overall, I can't say I recall a very amiable bunch of people from my time in Russia. They were not given to a friendly smile or wave for strangers on the street and were mostly scowling, especially while in the confines of a shared elevator. While they were never rude to us, we were treated very much as outsiders. Not partaking in the favourite local pastime of vodka meant we were also far removed from this aspect of social life in Moscow. Making friends may have proved tough as teetotalers but it did not take us long to feel at home in a city where Indian groceries and spices were easily available at one of the university shops. There were also occasional Indian musical performances sponsored by the Indian Embassy in Moscow, enjoyed also by local Russians. In fact, I recall watching some dubbed Hindi classics on Russian television – quite a memorable experience to watch the 1970s Bollywood classic 'Sholay' with Gabbar Singh spouting fluent Russian.

For our Russian to get to the level of following Gabbar's dialogues would take us a few years of intense twice-weekly lessons with our uncharacteristically friendly teacher. Learning the Cyrillic script proved extremely useful, from being able to read the road signs to the basic ingredients of items in the supermarket. Like most languages, it is important to master the grammar before being able to form logical sentences, given that the verbs are conjugated as in French and there are different gender references akin to Hindi.

Conversely, our Russian tutor's child wanted to make use of D'jemilla's teaching skills and learn English. Soon, her friend's son and our landlady's son Sergey joined in the Saturday morning English lessons with my wife at home. That was a special bond of friendship that formed over the course of our stay in Moscow, based on a mutual interest in each other's language skills and expanding to some cultural exchanges. It was thanks to our Russian tutor friend that we were introduced to the world-famous Russian ballet, with a performance of 'Swan Lake' at the Moscow City Ballet among the highlights of an overall fruitful Russian assignment, which our family cherishes to this day.

It is a reassuring thought that the enormous amount of goodwill created through the various community initiatives the AKF Representative Office was able to successfully operationalise in Russia continues to resonate despite the many political ups and downs and conflicts that were to come later.

Visits to communities to assess needs: Community in Gagarin and Lipidsk

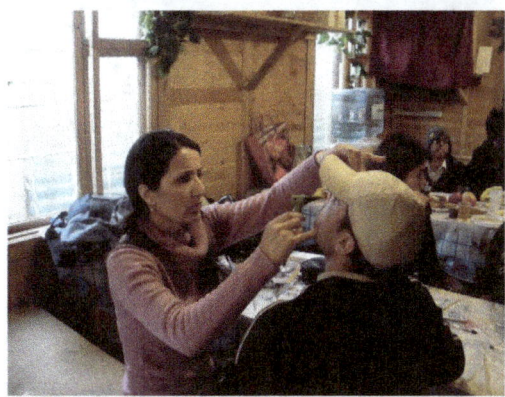

Ismaili Doctors Initiative (IDI)
visits to construction sites and annual meetings

*Reading for Children Programme:
Presentations to parents and training of facilitators*

*Civil Society Programme:
Meeting local leaders and English for volunteers*

*Youth camp
participants from Moscow and regions*

Chapter Four
Interventions of Compassion

Over the course of my career narrated in the previous chapters, there were some heart-wrenching natural disasters along the way that I was assigned to lead or assist as part of the emergency response coordinated by AKDN and FOCUS. These included devastating cyclones, floods, earthquakes and a tsunami in some of the toughest terrains. This chapter is a snapshot of what goes on behind the headline figures of the casualties and appeals for aid that are beamed around the world in the immediate aftermath.

MOZAMBIQUE – Cyclone Leon-Eline (2000)

When Mozambique was struck with catastrophic floods in the wake of the deadly Cyclone Leon-Eline in early 2000, I had just taken charge as Programme Manager for Afghanistan and was asked to rush over to the disaster zone in Southeast Africa.

At the time, I was very new to the humanitarian assistance landscape and had to quickly learn on the job as time was of the essence. I had just returned from my first assessment tour of Afghanistan *(Chapter 1)* and got a call the very next day that Mozambique's capital Maputo is to be my next destination, right away. My first thought was about getting a visa sorted and was relieved to find out that as a British passport holder, I could access a visa on arrival. Next on the list was some very speedy shopping in London to get waterproof clothing and boots to be prepared for the flood-hit country where thousands had been left homeless and in urgent need of the basic necessities of life.

The enduring and poignant image of a pregnant woman being rescued by a helicopter from a tree had already made an impact across television screens around the world at the time, symbolising the massive human toll and enormous scale of the disaster that was unfolding in the region.

His Highness had made a commitment to the then President, Jaoquim Chissano, and that's how the involvement of FOCUS Humanitarian Assistance in the flood relief efforts came about, in coordination with the United Nations (UN). A protocol had been signed with the Government of Mozambique in the late 1990s to assist and work in collaboration for the development of the country. This made my expedition our first intervention in the region, which piled on the added pressure of ensuring things went well with the aid mission as it would leave a lasting first impression for our future involvement in the development efforts of the country further down the road.

Mozambique, a former colony of Portugal, had very active Portuguese government support and assistance within hours of the cyclone hitting Africa. Our organisation in Lisbon had chartered a cargo plane packed with tents and inflatable boats, which we knew would be a basic requirement for those stranded in the floods to be evacuated to safety. The cargo also contained emergency medication, ready-to-eat canned food supplies including sardines and high energy biscuits and essential children's meals.

It was a team of four of us who then set off for Maputo, including some locals who spoke Portuguese – the lingua franca of Mozambique. Between me as an English speaker and these Portuguese speakers we were able to get by with some three-way translations involving English, Portuguese and the local African dialects. This presented its own set of challenges but at least it got things done. It spotlighted another beautiful aspect of our Ismaili community, how being multilingual helped us overcome some of these hurdles in times of crisis.

This proved all the more useful to me on this mission as I did not know anyone on the ground once I landed in the cyclone-ravaged country. My obvious first stop was our Jamatkhana, where I found the very welcome sight of a team of eager volunteers ready and primed for me to get into action. That meant a major chunk of my problem in this unknown territory was already solved, which was manpower.

The sourcing and packaging of food items was also already underway in the basement of the community centre which was our Jamatkhana.

The former First Lady and widow of ex-president Samora Machel, Graca Machel, was very active in the humanitarian arena and we went on to work closely with her over the course of this mission. As part of her tour of the various relief agencies, she was among our first visitors at the Jamatkhana on the very day I landed and was visibly pleased to see the progress of our relief efforts in such a short span of time.

Getting into Action

Feeling quite reassured on my arrival and raring to go, the next morning I made my way to the UN Disaster Assessment and Coordination (UNDAC) meeting, and I was faced with the reality of being somewhat of a late entrant to the relief efforts – this being AKDN's first intervention in the region. The local NGOs with an established base in the country were already way ahead in actioning their plans.

There was a massive operational map up on the wall highlighting the flood-hit areas and the agencies that had taken up the responsibility to serve specific spots, including the likes of Save the Children and World Vision, among others. I could see only a few zones that were yet to be assigned to any agency and I, rather ignorantly with very limited knowledge of the local terrain, offered to service the areas that were not yet being covered for humanitarian assistance. It soon became apparent why these zones had not yet been picked; it was because they had limited or zero access by road for the aid trucks to drive up with their supplies. This meant arduous boat rides across the flood-hit river waters in order to get to the people stranded in some of these extremely remote locations.

However, my rather foolhardy move in picking these inaccessible areas was to work in our favour eventually and give us a certain degree of first-mover advantage. My decision coincided with the South African government's announcement of a loan of a batch of military helicopters for use in the relief efforts, with a remit to help reach these inaccessible zones and to be coordinated by the UN's World Food Programme. While our team of volunteers got busy drafting plans for getting the aid trucks to the areas which had some road access and getting in place all the logistics of the quantity of supplies required, I approached the UN to seek the use of the helicopters for the areas that could be accessed only by air. This is where the first-mover advantage kicked in as we were given first dibs on the helicopters because we had volunteered to dispense aid to some of the remotest parts on the disaster map.

We secured two choppers for our supply chain and that's how our relief efforts quickly picked up speed – some truckloads being rolled out by road and the air drops being operationalised in parallel.

In this way, we were able to stick to our framework of providing aid directly to the beneficiaries without using intermediaries, ensuring the most equitable and fair distribution of life-saving supplies. Our process involved getting a list of the local households from the District Commissioners to tabulate each of the villages assessed as being most in need.

But the flip side of being the first also meant some very sharp learning curves along the way. I still remember my first aid helicopter ride because the chopper had to land in a makeshift patch of clay. Roughly five to-and-fro air trips were required for one truckload of supplies to be packed in and then offloaded at the other end. The first round of aid trucks was lined up extremely close to the muddy helicopter landing patch for the supplies to be loaded up as efficiently and quickly as possible for flight number one. Mindful of the limited flying time we may have before heavy rains scuppered the operation, we were keen to pack up the helicopters to their maximum load. But it soon became apparent that wasn't the smartest move because the helicopter began sinking under the weight of the load into the muddy patch. It was an important first lesson learned: the trucks cannot be parked so close to a fully loaded chopper as it would require greater force to achieve lift off, with the wings in danger of hitting the trucks in the process of such a shaky take-off. Once the trucks had been quickly ushered back to a safer distance, off we went to deliver the first consignment of much-needed aid.

On the other end, as the first helicopter load made its way to the remote spot, the locals had gathered and were patiently waiting for these supplies. Even as they ran towards us, there was no sense of chaos or mayhem among the crowds despite the desperate situation and we were able to set up a very organised distribution system. Under the watchful gaze of the District Commissioner, we set about matching up our lists with the supplies. The villagers who had travelled the farthest were served first, working our way down to those based closer to where the helicopter had landed, in order to create a fair and equitable distribution flow.

Soon, we had volunteers from the village joining in to give us a hand with operationalising a smooth system of names being called out and a thumbprint being taken to record the receipt of the supplies – a box of canned goods and some cooking essentials such as salt, sugar, cooking oil and a bag of maize flour to make the bread name *ugali* – a local staple. Photographs taken on these sites documented the efficiency of the process, both for our organisation and also for the district officials in charge.

At the end of five back and forth trips, our team packed into the empty helicopters for our return journey, leaving the last consignment to be distributed by the District Commissioner following the efficient system now in place. Local volunteers were well versed in this process by now, which was monitored efficiently by the villagers themselves to ensure no one attempted to access additional supplies that would deprive others yet to receive their quota.

Setting Up Base

The team I was leading was based at a hotel in Maputo being used by all humanitarian agencies and there were often days we were forced to spend within its confines, waiting for the incessant rains to subside to resume our supply operations. It was a kind of enforced lockdown due to the unusually heavy rainfall. I remember feeling very restless and frustrated when those rains just would not let up; it meant an enforced delay in getting food and shelter to the starving population. But perhaps, in hindsight, it was a useful break to catch up on much-needed sleep after the sheer intensity of the days spent coordinating and distributing the supplies.

Digital cameras were fairly new on the scene at the time and the not-so-smart mobile phones of the time with keyboards doubled up as a fax machine. One of my colleagues in the team that flew in with me from Portugal was adept at handling these gadgets, which proved very handy for our important admin tasks. I was able to send a report back to HQ every night, thanks to the ease of communication opened up by the developing technology – something we take so much for granted today.

Being a diverse and motley bunch also proved beneficial. The helicopter crew only spoke English, which meant I was the designated

English speaker and members of my team were able to help with the translations between them and the other local agencies who spoke either Portuguese or the local languages. This led to the World Food Programme later approaching FOCUS to help coordinate other operations involving the helicopter crew in other areas too. It went over and above our initial remit, but we were more than happy to be able to make a difference in every possible way at a time of such severe crisis. The volunteers were an extremely hard-working bunch, excited about their first helicopter rides while being at the forefront of making some crucial life-saving impact.

We soon distributed all the boats as required and the medications we had brought in were passed on to the Ministry of Health as donations for the flood victims because we weren't qualified to dispense these directly. We also had around 100 tents with us from Portugal and these we distributed in the north of the country in a town called Beira, where there was urgent need for shelter identified by the UN. For this mission, we were able to access a C-130 Hercules Army plane, and we coordinated with the NGO Shelter as part of a memorandum of understanding (MoU) with the UN for them to distribute the tents to the families rendered homeless by the floods.

That mission presented its own unique set of challenges because the plane had dropped us and our supplies and headed straight back to base. As we scrambled around to try and find our way back to

Maputo that evening, a local politician who had flown in for meetings in Beira kindly agreed to give us an airlift back to the capital after we explained why we were stranded on a runway late into the night.

One of the toughest trips I recall was a truck journey up to a boat and then an hour-long boat ride with the supplies to a remote, isolated island in the middle of nowhere. As we waited for the head of the village, I suddenly heard echoes of some chanting from a distance. Soon a vision emerged of a large group of women marching up, singing celebratory songs in their local language. I was informed they were singing in praise of the Lord because for them these supplies were a God send, a gift from heaven. The sensation of those rejoicing tunes lives on with me to this day. It was a sense of sheer joy and optimism amid all the desperation of a natural disaster, a celebration of getting some sustenance after countless days of enforced starvation.

Over the span of the three weeks I was in Mozambique, I executed a combination of these different means of getting the essentials to the flood victims. As an aside, Graca Machel had been approached by a church orphanage which was providing shelter to children orphaned in the floods and they hadn't received any rations due to their extremely inaccessible location. The only access route to get some basic supplies to them would have to be by air. So, she reached out to us and asked if FOCUS could assist with this intricate supply operation if she secured a government helicopter for us. We offered to step up and take on the responsibility with the help of a large Russian-built government chopper, which I was familiar with from my days in Tajikistan.

A military base was identified and off I went with my techie colleague, adept with the gadgets, to get things loaded before setting off for another remote destination. As soon as we landed at the orphanage, the nuns came rushing towards us and one of them hugged me to say, "you are an angel; God has answered our prayers". The memory of being referred to as God's angel fills me with emotion and brings tears to my eyes even now.

It was a fulfilling mission to see some reassurance in the eyes of the nearly 200 children seeking shelter there, a space which would have normally housed perhaps 20-30 inhabitants. The numbers had understandably swelled up as the natural disaster unfolded.

Hope Begins to Shine

In a crisis of this nature, the immediate focus is on distributing food, water and shelter and those action-packed three weeks were taken up in ensuring these were ticked off as best as possible. This being my very first on-ground humanitarian assistance mission, I learnt some very important lessons that would stand me in good stead in all my future assignments. There are four very well-known **C**s in our field: **C**oordination, **C**ooperation, **C**ommunication and **C**ollaboration.

They may sound very similar but when it comes to implementation, they are each very distinct and equally important steps.

I quickly learnt that "Coordination" must be at forefront, which is where important life-saving work begins to take shape as we coordinated with the UN, donors and other agencies, staying in constant "Communication" with all stakeholders. "Collaboration" with other NGOs, as we did with Shelter when distributing the tents, ensures there is no working at cross-purposes, and "Cooperation" with local authorities to reach the beneficiaries in need means each agency can add real value to the massive disaster response challenge before us.

The other encouraging realisation from my first such tour was of the extensive and energetic pool of volunteers from within our community who could be drawn upon in times of crises in different parts of the world. It meant a major aspect of the challenging task at hand was already covered: overcoming the need to seek out labour and manpower in unknown territories. Over the years, wherever I then went on new missions I had the reassuring sense that there were members of our community who were ready and willing to be harnessed for the greater good.

This was also my first face to face encounter with the desperation and despair that a natural disaster inflicts upon humans. But it is through this sense of despair that hope begins to shine through, as I witnessed in the uplifting chants of the women folk as they walked towards what they knew were food supplies to help alleviate their hunger; in the faces of the nuns at the orphanage who looked at us mere mortals as angels and very welcome conduits in their hour of need; and in the villagers who calmly queued for hours to receive their share of the supplies.

What I witnessed was that where there was darkness and dread, there is now hope! And that was a sight to behold each time we completed a treacherous journey to those remote rural areas, made even more isolated due to the devastating flood waters. These people could finally sense that they were isolated and alone no more, some help had finally arrived.

I also experienced first-hand how the international community rallies around in a crisis and got to observe the UN systems very closely, something that was to give me a head start time and time again in other disaster zones. Connections were made and rapports were built that would last through the course of my humanitarian work.

Having landed there with the brief to make sure FOCUS makes a good first impression in the region, it certainly felt like mission accomplished. We had gone above and beyond our initial remit and the geographical coverage of our relief efforts was quite wide as we reached out to populations in remote areas not being served by any other agencies.

As new, and somewhat later entrants, we had quickly established our reputation within the international aid community - as a rather small bunch of people who work closely together across different regions. From that first day when I looked at the UN operational map in the briefing room with names of international agencies serving the regions to the following weeks as FOCUS began delivering its aims - we were soon very firmly on the map! It was a proud moment to see FOCUS light up some of the most distant corners of Mozambique on that operational chart.

Three weeks later, when it was time for me to head out, we had certainly accomplished all that we had set out to, and more.

*Food Distribution:
Transported by air, by boat and by trucks*

INDIA – Earthquake in Bhuj, Gujarat (2001)

The disaster of the Bhuj earthquake in the Kutch district of the western Indian state of Gujarat in January 2001 hit very close to home for me in some ways. This was my ancestral region, a place I had never visited but always felt a strong tug towards. But destiny had decided that my first visit to the land of my forefathers was to be in a time of crisis, something I was plunged into quite unexpectedly.

As FOCUS Programme Manager of Programme Afghanistan, I was in Dubai racing against time to meet a deadline to submit a proposal to the United States Agency for International Development (USAID) related to our humanitarian work in Afghanistan. This was for a second food grant proposal for the then Taliban-controlled Afghanistan and Dubai was the neutral base chosen for all staff members operating out of Islamabad (Pakistan) and Khorog (Tajikistan) to fly in to and coordinate the submission.

However, due to some of the requisite visas not being processed in time, only my expatriate colleague from Khorog was able to join me in the Dubai office. From this temporary workspace loaned to us by the Ismaili community, we set about working manically to meet the midnight of 26 January 2001 deadline for the submission of the grant proposal. The task at hand of coordinating and collating the rudimentary information pouring in from different sources through satellite phone data was a rather complex one. But we were determined to get this done in time and worked non-stop overnight to get it drafted and submitted just before midnight Washington time.

In the early hours of the morning, as we breathed a sigh of relief after a job well done in our opinion, my colleague and I headed to a nearby American diner to grab a quick breakfast bite before some much-needed sleep.

Horror Unfolds

Just as we settled down and ordered our meal, I happened to glance at the large television screen in the diner which was flashing the news of a devastating earthquake that had struck Gujarat – with its epicentre in Bhuj.

The horrific footage of destruction and loss of life shook me to the core as I turned to my Canadian colleague, Nooramin, to say this is in Gujarat where my familial roots lie. Members of our Ismaili community were among the thousands impacted by the disaster, it soon emerged. I immediately called our Global Office Coordinator, who answered with an anxious 'Farid, where are you?' Turns out, they had been trying to connect with me with a response strategy already being drawn up after His Highness had made an immediate commitment to the government of India of humanitarian assistance.

The quake-hit families had spent their first night outdoors in bitter cold conditions, making shelter the utmost urgency in the cold January nights of Gujarat. In a way, it was fortuitous that I was in Dubai which is just over a three-hour flight from India, and I was asked to begin sourcing as many tents as possible and make my way to Bhuj.

My brief, understandably, was that I had to get there as quickly as possible before the stranded families are forced to spend another night out in the cold. I set about my mission in a completely sleep-deprived state – not having slept the previous night due to the submission deadline – but there was simply no time to dwell on such matters.

Over the next few hours, a series of fortunate set of events were to help make this enormous task at hand just that little bit easier. For a start, it so happened that just a few weeks ago our local Ismaili community health committee, led by a friend named Salim Hadi, had been involved in assisting the Canadian Embassy with their famous annual charity event known as the Terry Fox Run. This meant they were well acquainted with the suppliers of the kind of large tents that would be required for my Bhuj mission, having ordered them for their first aid and water posts along the route of the run recently. The vetting process of narrowing down the most efficient and cost-effective suppliers had already taken place, making our task that much quicker as members of the Health Committee had offered to assist with the procurement and were delegated that particular task. Meanwhile, I set about sorting out my Indian visa and reached out to the Indian Embassy in Dubai. Again, fortune was in my favour as the Ambassador personally intervened, inviting us into his office right away because he was aware of His Highness' commitment to the government. That was probably one of the quickest visa stamps I have ever had in my passport, sorted out by the Ambassador himself.

Looking back, I can't help but wonder that there certainly was a divine helping hand at work against the backdrop of a natural disaster. Everyone seemed fully geared up to cooperate and assist, from lining up the tents to paving the way for them to get to their destination. Given the large consignment on our hands, we began exploring the various options of getting them to their destination – by road would simply take too long; dhows using the water route between Dubai and India would also not serve our purpose as that would take multiple days too; and a regular cargo plane would not suffice in terms of the space required for our large tent consignment, besides the added hassle of the freight paperwork involved.

It was a race against the clock as we weighed up these different options, all the time mindful that soon it would be nightfall again for the thousands rendered homeless by the quake and its aftershocks. In yet another sign of fortune favouring our endeavours, the local community leaders managed to charter a massive Russian cargo plane – an Illusion-76 (a.k.a. Soviet Beast IL-76), which is equipped to carry freight as large as battle tanks and has a massive weight allowance of around 50 tonnes. Our freight comprised of 500 solid quality, insulated tents designed to shield against tough weather conditions, and some blankets, gloves for the rescue workers to sift through the rubble, all of which fell well within the IL-76 specifications. Meanwhile, our community leaders were coordinating the collection of the tents from the various suppliers using trucks loaned from contacts to get the consolidated shipment to the Dubai cargo section of the airport for me to then set off with the consignment.

Lost in Translation

A small snag arose when the airport authorities, and rightly so for security reasons, said only their authorised personnel could enter the premises to load these tents onto the plane. Given the urgency of the operation, they assured us that the process would be completed at the earliest which would allow us to take off in the early hours for Ahmedabad (Gujarat), the closest airport to the epicentre of Bhuj.

At this stage, I probably looked like a walking zombie, having already skipped one whole night and day's sleep, heading into a second night without any sleep. It was in this state of mind that I was eventually directed by the pilot to a side door of the massive beast of an aircraft to climb up a precarious step ladder and then jump in using a rope dangling next to it.

Now, this assignment coming years before my Russian posting, I was at a language disadvantage, and it was only through some gestures that I gathered that I was expected to use this knotty rope to take my place, sandwiched in the crunched-up space between the five-member flying crew in the cockpit in front of me and the baggage hold behind me. Most certainly a flight to remember, with no question of any seatbelts or flight safety protocols. My zombie self was soon perched on a flimsy plastic chair, the variety we would expect to see in a garden rather than as a passenger seat on an aircraft. But I was in no fit state to contemplate any of the safety implications and simply grabbed a second chair to place my legs on before nodding off.

It was probably for the best that it was in this drowsy state that I experienced the rather unusual take off, with my chairs sliding along in line with captain's manoeuvres and then back into place once we were airborne. A rather different kind of daring funfair ride, very much suspended in mid-air, I thought. By now, fatigue had taken complete hold of my mind, and I was soon knocked out into a deep sleep.

It must have been half-way through our journey that I felt being shaken vigorously by one of the crew members and he was repeating the phrase "No Ahmedabad, No Ahmedabad". For a second, I wondered if this was a dream but turned out it wasn't. After much back and forth of broken English, he asked me to follow him to the cockpit, which meant a frightening vertigo inducing walk over the glass-bottomed IL-76.

The navigator, who spoke a little English, conveyed to me that we can't actually land in Ahmedabad due to heavy air traffic caused by aid flights from domestic and international airports converging upon the airport, ruling out runway space for us any time soon. He offered me two options: to fly back to Dubai and await a landing spot in Ahmedabad or divert to Mumbai. Heading back was simply not an option, given the urgency of the crisis, so I decisively told them it would have to be option two.

The moment my plane touched down in Mumbai, my mobile phone – one of those models that predated today's smartphones – lit up with multiple missed calls. Our team had obviously been apprised of this last-minute diversion and were desperately trying to map my journey to Bhuj from Mumbai, a few extra miles added on to the originally intended Ahmedabad-Bhuj journey by road.

The then President of the Ismaili Council for India, Hamida Allana, had arranged matters with the aviation authorities and was trying to reach me to let me know that she had organised a fleet of volunteers to help with the offloading of the cargo planes jamming the

Ahmedabad landing strip as part of a wider fast-tracking system for my onward journey to the city. The whole process took a few hours and on arrival of our shipment, around 15 trucks were lined up to be loaded from the IL-76, with me providing regular updates to our Global Office Coordinator, Anar. The plan was for us to arrive in Ahmedabad later than initially planned, in the evening, with a view that I would check into a hotel before setting off for Bhuj early the next morning once the cargo had been loaded by staff now freed up from the airport backlog. However, given that the families in Bhuj had now already spent a couple of nights out in the cold without any shelter, my instructions were to start the road journey right away in the very early hours of the morning, in order to get the supplies intended for the villages, towns and cities around the epicentre of the earthquake.

There were reports of roads and bridges being damaged along the route and, in some instances, aid trucks being marauded by the displaced people desperate for some basic sustenance. But despite the night-time dangers, there was no time to be lost in trying to get to our final destination. We stopped over at a roadside *dhaba*, very basic eateries along motorways in India, where I had one of my most memorable breakfasts. After many hours of starvation, an unhygienically cooked omelette and an over sweetened cup of *chai* (tea) felt like a real feast.

Then it was time to squeeze back into a Maruti Suzuki, one of those dinky cars that were ubiquitous in India at the time but clearly not designed for anyone above very average height. I somehow managed to fold my legs into the back seat and we set off, with the trucks trailing the car in a convoy that was instructed to regroup at a few stops along the way for safety reasons. On this never-ending journey, we encountered some added roadblocks due to the visit of the state's Chief Minister who was on a tour of the quake-hit villages the same day.

Meanwhile, Anar kept frantically calling me to check the progress of our journey because our aim was to try and get there before the displaced people had to endure another night of feeling abandoned outdoors. Eventually, we drove into Bhuj late into the night and set up base at the grounds of the boy's hostel in the city, not habitable indoors due to the damage by the quake and where the boys and local residents had made makeshift sleeping arrangements outdoors.

Members of our community had set up an outdoor communal kitchen to try and offer some sustenance to those affected in the neighbourhood. I recall a very inexplicable sense of homecoming as someone who spoke the local Kutchi/Gujarati and came face to face with an elderly lady, who was lamenting the city's fate and questioning why God had brought this suffering upon their homes. The scene that

I encountered on that first night was one of sheer desperation, tears and trauma of the people who had lost loved ones or suffered severe injuries and, in many cases, lost all their earthly possessions.

That night, I became one of them and slept outdoors, albeit using the car for some shelter. I saw families shivering like me as they huddled together under a blanket for some warmth and security, with little babies bawling into the night. There was despair all around but, unfortunately, their temporary shelter that had been flown in many miles would have to wait another few hours for the first signs of daylight.

None of the buildings, including the youth hostel, were habitable for fear of aftershocks. Being at the epicentre of the earthquake as we were, these shaky buildings and precariously leaning structures could wreak further havoc and had to be left abandoned. So, there was no option but to be out in the open.

Operation Shelter

Finally, it was sunrise and the volunteers who had come in from different parts of the state and surrounding areas, even further afield from Sidhpur and Mumbai, together with colleagues Galib and Faiza who had flown in from FOCUS in Pakistan gathered around to get the first camp up and running on the very field which had been our open-air sleeping area overnight. Two-three of the tents were combined to create a large multi-purpose community shelter that could be used for congregational prayers, briefings, support for children and psychosocial counselling for the post-traumatic stress the citizens were understandably suffering from.

All this was being organised at speed, with some volunteers also busy setting up a functional kitchen with basic cooking facilities, organising fuel and food supplies. At the end of that first day, there was a near miraculous transformation from the despair of night before when I first drove in. There was a palpable shift in the perspective of the locals; from lamenting their fate and look back at the past, they were now looking ahead at what needed doing. I was now face to face with the sheer force of human resilience and the capacity of human nature to fight back once there is a sense that they are not alone.

The chorus around me had changed to one of optimism, with people thankful to God for ensuring there was help at hand in the face of disaster. They were not alone in this time of despair because assistance was being organised. The shift in the mindset, being encouraged by the community leaders, was to try and organise things to move towards some semblance of normality and begin reconstructing lives. Setting up shelter in such disaster zones is not just about the tents. Ensuring a safe source of drinking water, preventing water-borne and other diseases, organising electricity for these temporary tent-homes to bring some respite in the long, dark nights were all part of the early response protocol for the camps.

The tents were distributed based on the needs of the local communities, with some local shopkeepers utilising theirs to set up shop in an effort to get the local economy up and running again, at least to some degree. In the uncertainty that looms in the immediate aftermath of an earthquake of such a massive scale, even people whose homes have sustained only partial damage are forced into the tents until it is safe to return to the concrete structures once the tectonic plates have settled following the many aftershocks that are to be expected in the wake of an earthquake.

As a result, I oversaw several such camps being set up in the span of the 10 days I was there, starting with Bhuj, Nagalpur and Kera among some of the villages in the area covered with anywhere between five and 75 tents in each location. Incidentally, Nagalpur is famous for its semolina-based sweet, known as *seero* or *halwa*, the taste of which I recall with much warmth. This was also my first taste of the food of the land where my roots lay, and this very first visit certainly impacted each of my senses.

After the initial days, the focus turned from the basic food and shelter needs towards addressing the wider mental and physical health requirements. Setting up male and female toilet facilities, water tankers for drinking water, creating an education routine for the children and providing them and their parents with psychosocial care were all important for the population to start finding a rhythm to their lives once again. My own routine was setting in – taking pictures on my Sony digital camera and keeping the Global Office updated about the progress of the camps. The base was in Bhuj, where my "bedroom" was to be the tent which when I dosed off would have a handful of people and by the time I woke up, would have 10-15 volunteers huddled up to shelter from the cold. As I would make my daily visits to the surrounding areas to see the progress of our camps, I was always struck by the very visible transformation from despair to hope.

Gone was the despondency and in its place was a sense of determination to look ahead to the future and get life back to some semblance of normality. At night, the sounds of wailing had soon given way to some laughter. The congregational prayers gave our community a lot of solace, with people of different religious affiliations similarly finding their own sanctuary in their places of worship within this tight-knit community. The neighbourly bonds were very heartening to see, irrespective of any religious or class divides. As I was constantly showered with an overwhelming sense of gratitude from the locals, I found myself always pointing to the inspiring organisation and His Highness' vision behind these efforts.

This was my second humanitarian mission, and I felt better equipped than my first assignment in Mozambique. And, of course, there was that strong connect and a sense of being rooted to this region, able to speak the language and a strong sense that I was one of them. I remember someone offering to dig up more about my familial roots but at the time, my single-minded focus was on getting the camps organised at speed. Now, in hindsight, I wish I had taken up that offer – very much along the lines of the popular BBC show 'Who Do You Think You Are?'

That first visit to India left an indelible mark, encountering some of the most resourceful people I have had the fortune to meet and work with. There was a sense of just getting on with things and not waiting for help to land on their doorsteps, no matter the scale of the disaster. Over the years, this is something I found lies at the core of human nature – life does go on, be it in the midst of wars or natural disasters, human resilience and civil society finds a way to shine through. The feeling of a "helping hand" always guiding and providing comfort to humanity.

All those warnings of marauders targeting aid convoys never did come to pass and my experience was a very positive one, with no negatives hindering the task at hand. The communities came together to pitch in as best as possible because each member felt they had a stake in the rebuilding of their lives in the aftermath of this terrible tragedy.

What a journey this was, from sheer despair to hope for the brighter days that lay ahead.

Destruction of homes and cultural assets

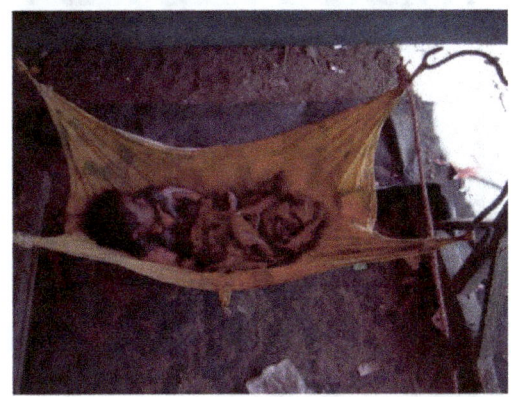
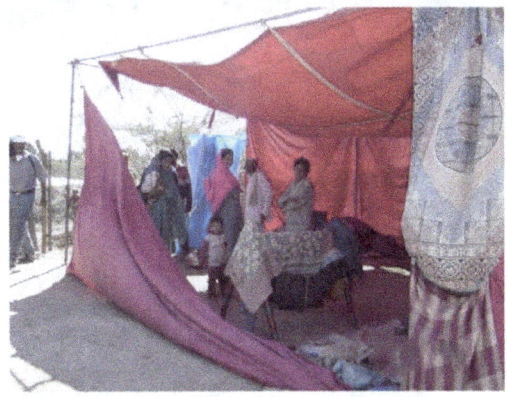

Makeshift homes and shops

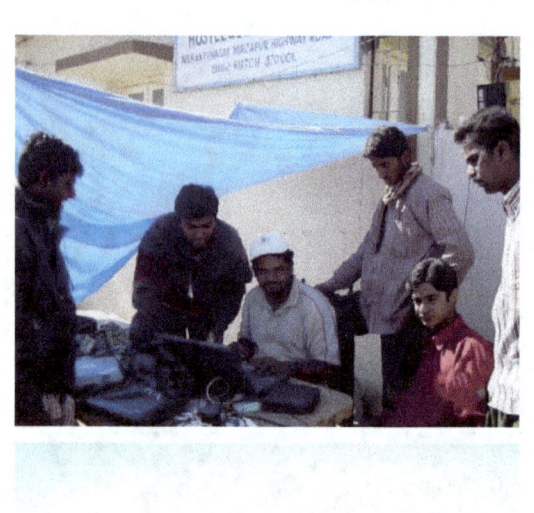

Planning and set-up of camps

Water supply, electricity and communal dining

On-site health care, and planning next steps with communities

Faces of hope

Boxing Day Tsunami (2004)

The catastrophe of the Boxing Day Tsunami, described as the worst natural disaster in modern times, struck the Indian Ocean in December 2004 and devastated communities along the entire coastline, including several coastal regions of southern India. I happened to be on holiday with my family in Kenya at the time and remember following the news of the disaster from there. I had completed my term as Programme Manager, Programme Afghanistan, and was back in the FOCUS Europe London office as the Global Crisis Response Coordinator – a role which involved coordinating and undertaking training in crisis planning and management.

By 2004, we had a considerable FOCUS presence in India, headquartered in Mumbai, and the very accomplished team dived into the immediate relief and rescue efforts, boosting the work of the local government and NGOs distributing food and non-food items and organising much-needed psychosocial counselling for the communities. My involvement in these efforts, therefore, took on a very different role to my first visit to India three years earlier as part of the immediate disaster response to the Bhuj earthquake.

The remit by the time I was dispatched a few weeks after the tsunami in January 2005 was to boost the psychosocial counselling and assess the requirements from a long-term rehabilitation perspective for the communities supported by our First Response unit. The Aga Khan Foundation (AKF) was to then step in with a recovery and development plan for these affected areas in the state of Andhra Pradesh, southern India, based on our assessments.

In Hyderabad, now part of the adjoining state of Telangana, a new Aga Khan Academy was in the offing and, in keeping with our development ethos, AKDN was exploring other avenues of support critical to the surrounding villages and towns in the aftermath of the massive loss of life and livelihood caused by the tsunami. Our longer-term development efforts would therefore be tailored to help the affected communities rebuild their lives and get back into their vocation – in this case largely fishing – as soon as possible.

I was joined by another colleague, Salim, on what was to be my second tour of India to assess how our humanitarian assistance could be boosted and to lay the groundwork for AKF's proposed initiatives in the region. We flew into the Indian capital of Delhi, where we had a meeting scheduled with the AKF team before making our way to Hyderabad. A train and then a car journey brought us to Krishna, which was to be our base for the week-long visit. There is one thing that I do remember clearly from the train journey: as we were chugging along, enjoying the views or dozing off into short naps, I heard a voice that sounded like "Soup" and lo and behold it was a vendor selling soup. It was more out of curiosity than a craving or hunger that I purchased this soup. It was served in a thermal cup, piping hot, and tasted like any other tomato soup. It felt like quite the local quirk that train passengers had the option to purchase such items besides the usual tea, coffee and soft drinks. I realised it was the norm and soon there were vendors selling all sorts of food and non-food items at the short station stops on the way – ranging from boiled eggs, savoury snacks, sweet meats to flasks, balloons, toys and miscellaneous thrifty gift items; you name it, they had it.

On the Ground

The FOCUS India team had coordinated a very thorough response within hours of the disaster, establishing their base at Machilipatnam in the Krishna district of Andhra Pradesh with the help of volunteers drawn from different parts of the country. Besides distributing packets of food to sustain the devastated families, the volunteers had also distributed items such as blankets, clothing and sheets for makeshift shelter.

The FOCUS India team involved in psychosocial counselling also joined us and my colleague with expertise in this area was advising them on those aspects. As soon as we had checked into our hotel, we were to join these teams and get started. However, there was another surprise in store for me before we set out for our meetings and field visits. Due to the standard rooms at the hotel being overbooked, I was upgraded to the "Honeymoon Suite" which had an unusually round bed, such that I had probably seen only in Bollywood movies.

On my first field visit I was struck by how, even after a few weeks of the disaster, the intensity of the tsunami remained apparent. The water levels were still very high, coming into the villages way past where their boats were usually moored at the edge of the water, with broken fishing nets and boats strewn all over the place completing the woeful signs of destruction. We had all read about and watched the scenes of the devastation unfold on our television screens as villages were swept away and submerged but to inspect the scene as an eyewitness is something else altogether. Several coconut trees had been swept away and of those that survived, their trunks were barely visible over the extremely high tide.

The entire world was shaken up by the Boxing Day Tsunami of 2004 because it accentuated the devastating impact of a tsunami into our vocabularies, alongside the more common disasters such as earthquakes and floods. The trauma it left in its wake was there for us to see in those villages we toured in Andhra Pradesh. Families were still struggling to come to terms with the loss of their near and dear ones and very gradually trying to move towards rebuilding their lives.

Unlike my visit to Gujarat where I knew the language, this was a different landscape where the local Telugu language and its dialects were completely alien to me and the food, of course, also entirely different with *dosas* (Indian pancakes) for breakfast in this part of the country. Our local volunteers helped with the interpretation as we undertook our surveys with people whose hard graft in their daily lives was etched on their faces.

We kick-started with a meeting with the District Collector, the senior official in charge of the area, who was very familiar with FOCUS as his office had doubled up as a base for our volunteers during their humanitarian response in the immediate aftermath of the disaster. This was followed up by meetings with village elders and community leaders as we drove to some of the impacted regions on the coastline as part of our assessment of what the locals were in dire need of. These visits highlighted not only the sheer force with which the tsunami struck but also the suddenness of its impact on a region accustomed to and therefore quite prepared for cyclones. The local fisherfolk were geared towards heeding to early warnings and had several cyclone shelters created for the coastal families to seek refuge in.

However, the unprecedented nature of a disaster of the scale of the tsunami was starkly on display in one village where the cyclone shelter was being used as a cow shed – that's just how unexpected even a life-threatening cyclone had become to them. But it was obvious that even if this shelter was not being used to house the cows, it would have offered little relief from the sheer force with which the waves struck this part of the coastline.

We set about making notes with the help of the villagers on how they had lost all their sources of income, which was dominated by aquaculture – fishing and shellfish farming – and some coconut cultivation. We were also told how the mangrove plantations had protected some of the villages from complete devastation, having served as a natural barrier to the flood waters. Our assessment was that the priority was to help those whose boats and fishing nets had been damaged or lost. Additionally, some support for them to re-start their small-scale businesses of making and repairing fishing nets was to be on the list of recommendations to get the local economy back on its feet through support for each link in the supply chain.

The plantation of mangrove forests as an insurance policy against future tsunamis was also included in the report, filed for the longer-term development initiatives and handed over to the leadership in Mumbai for onward transmission to AKF to eventually take on board and action as deemed feasible for the region. The damage done by the tsunami was extensive and it was clear that multiple agencies would have to work in tandem to help those impacted overcome their trauma and rebuild their lives.

Ironically, the very ocean which was their source of life and livelihood had wreaked such devastation on them. But the sheer force of human resilience was once again very apparent as these hardworking folk set about rebuilding their lives from scratch after it was all swept away by the magnitude of the shock waves.

Long-Term Vision

It is heartening to know that these initial recommendations would go on to become a part of AKF's ongoing development initiatives in the region. The Aga Khan Academy, Hyderabad, is today a centre of excellence which is available for means-tested students from all over India to provide education opportunities for children of all backgrounds. Admittedly, I am particularly biased given that my youngest son benefitted from the world-class education offered by one such academy in Mombasa, Kenya, when we were based in Russia.

High Highness has a vision to have "an integrated network of schools to be located in countries across Africa, South and Central Asia, and the Middle East". It has led to operational academies in India, Kenya, Mozambique and Bangladesh offering full scholarships to excellent students who may not be able to afford higher education otherwise.

On a personal level, my tour of Andhra Pradesh incorporated my first experience of undertaking a mission of this nature – beyond the first response after a natural disaster to drawing up the framework for longer term rehabilitation and development of an affected region. Once again, I was in the fortunate position to see desperation give way to a hopeful future.

Distribution of essentials, psychosocial counselling and meeting communities

Kashmir Earthquake (2005)

On 8 October 2005, a disastrous earthquake struck the region of Kashmir with territories on both sides of the Line of Control (LoC) between India and Pakistan severely impacted - the epicentre being Muzaffarabad, falling under the latter's administration.

While a major joint FOCUS Humanitarian Assistance and AKDN relief effort was mounted to assist with the devastation on the Pakistani side - which suffered massive destruction of homes, public buildings and communication networks, I was deputed to the Indian side of the LoC to assess and initiate the humanitarian assistance alongside the FOCUS India team for the families affected in some of the remotest parts of the mountainous terrain. I was based at the London office at the time, handling the Crisis Response Management, and quickly set about organising my visa for what would be my third visit to India. The remit was for FOCUS to undertake the immediate response efforts, which would then be followed up by potential long-term development initiatives by AKF, based on some of our early assessments on the ground.

Therefore, within days of the quake I was on a flight from London to Delhi, where members of the FOCUS India team had gathered from Mumbai and were waiting for me to land in time to catch the connecting flight to Srinagar - the capital of the then state of Jammu and Kashmir (J&K) and today known as Union Territories. By the time I landed at the international terminal of Delhi Airport, the flight to Srinagar from the domestic terminal some miles away was ready to take off. Desperate pleas from the FOCUS team about our humanitarian mission somehow managed to hold the plane for just enough time for me to be bussed over and rushed through immigration to ensure we weren't pushed behind schedule.

Once we landed in Srinagar, I recall being struck by the efficiency and organisational expertise of our FOCUS India team, which was functioning like a well-oiled machine by this time. All the basics of setting up our base in the city and getting the local communication networks in place with the requisite mobile phone SIM cards was done at record speed and our team of five was fully geared up to get started to boost the relief efforts.

The key problem already identified by the team was of shelter, especially in the context of the harsh winter weather conditions that would soon intensify for the quake-hit families whose homes had been destroyed. The Mumbai team had already been in the process of acquiring several winterised tents, strongly insulated and waterproof to shield against the elements, based on some provisional numbers. So, our first stop was to touch base with the Indian Army officers who oversaw all operations in this part of Kashmir.

We started off with a meeting fixed with the help of one of our team members, Nagma, who had familial contacts within the local Army base. We sought advice on the requirements on the ground and how we should go about facilitating this through the relevant local contacts. This initial meeting established that one of the areas badly hit by the quake was the town of Uri in Baramulla district of Kashmir and while relief efforts were ongoing, there were further requirements of shelter for the affected families. Food provisions were being coordinated by the Army and they welcomed any support to boost the shelter requirements.

On the Road

Once we had a contact point in Uri, nearly two hours' drive from Srinagar, we hit the road to get started on our mission. The person waiting for us there turned out to be very welcoming and helpful, appreciative of our efforts as a not-for-profit and apolitical agency there to assist the Army in its relief efforts.

We presented our plan to support with the provision of winterised support packages, including tents, blankets and sweaters. The way we prepared our distribution plan was to create family kits, enough for around 1,000 families (around 5,000 people) prioritising female-headed households with dependent elderly folk and children. Next in line were families who had suffered a fatality in the earthquake and finally the poverty-stricken households with more than three children under our identified criteria. These lists were drafted alongside the local village *sarpanch* (chieftain) and the area's Army Commanding Officer (CO), Colonel P.K. Singh, with the underlying principle remaining the same as in all our disaster response – ensuring the aid is delivered directly to the beneficiaries without the involvement of intermediaries.

Each of the "Family Kits" contained a similar set of provisions:

- One winterised tent that slept five
- Five sweaters of different sizes – two adults and three children
- Five blankets
- Five pairs of socks
- Five winter caps, known locally as "monkey caps"
- Five pairs of Wellies or snow boots

We set about in a hired 4X4 to visit the six villages identified by Col. Singh as the ones most in need of these kits – with villages Sarai, Jabra, Chapar and Sahadara the first four that were priorised for immediate relief. Our assessment revealed that at least 600 homes were severely damaged in these areas and these were the households we offered our kits to one by one. This took us nearly a week, going into each village, setting up contact with the *sarpanch* and creating a list of beneficiaries.

The sheer force of the earthquake, even days after the tremors had subsided, was not only visible in the debris of the homes it destroyed but also on the faces of the families left homeless. These were inhabitants accustomed to the harsh climes of the region, but the additional force of Mother Nature's fury had left them completely devastated. The sense of isolation was enhanced by the very remote location of the rural terrain, bereft of the hustle and bustle of urban centres. The makeshift shelters they had built using their ingenuity with whatever they could find, including some abandoned wood and corrugated tin roofs shattered in the quake, were not only inadequate but also a health and safety risk.

These were not densely populated areas, which meant long journeys up into the mountains to ensure all the small tenements dotted across were covered and no one got left behind without the help they so urgently needed before the temperatures dropped below zero and snow made matters even worse. The other logistics nightmare we were dealing with was flying in the tents procured by the team in Mumbai to Srinagar. Here, once again the Russian IL-76 Soviet Beast military aircraft came in handy to get the gear flown over by the Indian Air Force (IAF). The need that the armed forces had identified for the region was for 30,000 winterised tents, 17,000 of which had already been met by the Army response units and we further bolstered these with 1,000 tents and family kits.

During my 10-day mission in the region, I was able to directly oversee the launch of this process with 200 kits distributed right away to families from four villages – the most isolated and least winterised relief serviced – with the remaining overseen by the team over the course of the next few days. Our well established and streamlined system was set in motion, with the villagers identified on our lists informed by their local *sarpanch* to head towards the distribution point adjacent to the military helipad at Sultandaki in Uri – at an elevation of 3,000 metres – from where the kits, now trucked over to a storage facility from the airport, were ready to be handed out.

This is where education as one of the key future development needs of the region came into sharp focus for me, as most of the villagers were only equipped to use their thumbprints rather than a signature on the documents confirming receipt of their aid packages. They came with their mules or wheelbarrows, and if they couldn't afford mules for longer distance journeys, we helped hire one for them to be able to cart their kits back to their remote villages up the mountainous trek.

On my final day, our FOCUS vice-chair flew in from Bangalore (now Bengaluru) to assess the work on the ground and I had the privilege of visiting some of the families now secure in their new winterised tents. The refrain from many was of deep gratitude, expressing their relief at the fact their children would now have some warm clothing and shelter for the harsher winter months ahead, until they are able to rebuild a more permanent home.

Our final assessment for the longer-term work to be undertaken by AKF had a three-pronged focus: meeting the lack of education support, enhancing the healthcare provisions, and assistance to revive the rural economy.

Once again, I was very moved by the human resilience that we encountered in this tough mountainous terrain. We have all read and heard much about the stunning beauty of Kashmir, often referred to as "paradise on earth", and I had the fortune to witness this with my own eyes. In fact, when the local hotel was over-subscribed, some of us had to relocate to a houseboat on the famed Dal Lake and that remains an experience I will never forget. It is here that I encountered my first experience of floating markets, with the Kashmiris carrying on their local trade in just about everything from these boats – from fruits and vegetables to shawls and jewellery. I recall the excitement of a teenager I experienced when the houseboat in which the Beatles stayed during their visit to Kashmir in the 1960s was pointed out, just a few boats down from mine.

The tragedy of the decades-old political conflict in this region, disputed between India and Pakistan, was compounded by the natural disaster but the robustness of these hardy folk shone through as we toured the region. Fortunately, we did not encounter any strife or threats during our mission, but the sense of tension was all pervasive because a bomb going off somewhere was not that uncommon in this strife-torn landscape.

A sense that life must go on with as much normality as possible soon became very palpable during my stay in the heavily militarised zone. By the time it was time to leave Kashmir, I had a feeling of satisfaction that we had been able to help at least some impacted Kashmiris face the brutal winter just around the corner with at least a little warmth; their anguish giving way to some hope in this conflict-prone territory.

Destruction and makeshift shelter

Relief arrives at distribution point

Verification and distribution

Back to their plot of land

Faces of hope

MADAGASCAR – Cyclone Gafilo (2004)

In the year 2004, when Cyclone Gafilo struck Madagascar, I was in London supporting Crises Planning and Crisis Management globally. The eastern and north-eastern part of the island was the worst impacted, causing destruction at a massive and unprecedented scale.

Madagascar being a French-speaking island meant that FOCUS Europe's French wing took charge of the humanitarian efforts. Our Ismaili Community Council, based in the capital Antananarivo – commonly referred to as Tana, were asked to oversee the implementation work. As they would require some technical on-ground support, I was asked to make my way to Tana and assist with the UN coordinated relief efforts. Based on an understanding, FOCUS was to partner with the Catholic Relief Services (CRS) as the local agency with a base in Tana and this was to prove a very impactful tie-up from the moment I connected with their team to take stock of the situation and join the UN relief efforts.

I flew to Madagascar via Paris and encountered the oddest of welcomes as soon as I stepped out into the arrivals hall with my field gear. A lady rushed forward to garland me with flowers, leaving me bemused about whether this was a local tradition I had not been briefed about. The President of our Ismaili Council who was there to collect me saw this from a distance and observing my discomfort, had a chat with the lady in French to ascertain that the garland was not in fact intended for me. They were at the airport to receive a gentleman who was to wed their daughter and it being a match arranged remotely, this was the first time the family was to meet the groom. As I walked out dressed in my customary formal attire of jacket and trousers in readiness for any formal meetings at the Jamatkhana, the wedding party presumed I was that very groom they had organised the welcome party for! It was quite the welcome, one that isn't easily forgotten. Of course, I did politely return their garland so it could be passed on to the intended recipient.

We had a good laugh about it on the way to the Jamatkhana, where the serious work of taking stock and preparing a strategy began right away. The havoc wreaked by Cyclone Gafilo was playing out on the television screens, with the roofs blown off major buildings including many schools. As we reviewed some of the videos of the damage, it became clear that rehabilitating some of the schools should also be on top of our agenda. And, over time, the rehabilitation of two school buildings was completed as Phase 2 of the relief efforts.

There was a long-term vision at play here, to make contacts within the Ministry of Education to show them that our agency was here for the long haul. AKDN had plans to set up an academy in Madagascar, same as in Mozambique, and this would lay the groundwork and demonstrate our commitment to the country. The following day we touched base with CRS and headed to the UN coordination meeting together. We discovered that CRS had enough food supplies and UNICEF had the required kits known as "School in a Box" for children to continue their education in disaster zones. The problem was they didn't have the means to get these to the victims due to a shortage of trucks and fuel for the trucks.

Coincidentally, or serendipitously, many of the local Ismaili community members' businesses involved transportation and many others ran petrol stations. Our partnership with CRS would, therefore, prove quite effective – they provided the food, and we stepped in with the means to transport it to the beneficiaries. The contribution of FOCUS then was determined as hiring the trucks, buying the fuel those vehicles would require and distributing to locations underserved or not served at all. There were also some inaccessible areas to factor in, where these trucks would not be of much use. Just in time, as they had done in Mozambique, the South African government donated two helicopters to support the relief efforts in Madagascar under a regional cooperation agreement.

We now had a clear strategy based on my earlier experiences, identifying areas where the trucks could get to and where the helicopters would be deployed from our Majunga base in the northeast of the island – famous for its welcoming Baobab tree, sandy beaches and glorious sunsets. The volunteers worked with great efficiency, and we were able to distribute the food supplied by CRS – with our banners reflecting the joint effort of Catholic Relief Services and FOCUS Humanitarian Assistance. For the children's kits and supplies we distributed, the stickers read: donated by UNICEF, distributed by FOCUS Humanitarian Assistance. It was a symbol of a very productive partnership between different agencies coming together to fulfil a common goal.

This coordination also resonated more widely as the South African helicopters came with the same crew who we had worked with in Mozambique. So, we were able to build on that rapport and help translate between French and the Gujarati used by our Ismaili community, which I was familiar with.

Help at Hand

This breaking down of language barriers helped a great deal as we did our sorties with the supplies. It was to also prove useful when one of the two helicopters malfunctioned on the way back to collect us from a remote village. A colleague and I waited in vain after we had finished distributing the supplies.

As it started to get dark in this unknown territory, without any satellite phone, mobile signal or other means of communication, the panic began to set in. We spotted a small general store, which happened to be run by a family of Indian heritage, just like me, who spoke Gujarati! They confirmed our worst fears that there was no connectivity by road for us to be able to get back to base and the only means of communication would be to access the District Commissioner's VHF Radio (walkie-talkie). The official very kindly put out an SOS message on our behalf, which was picked up by a ship in the sea who we requested to contact our base. That is how we discovered that our helicopter had broken down and was definitely not on its way back to collect us. The only option available to us was to be picked up by car from a specified point where the dust road, or what was left of it, connected to a main road – the coordinates of which we hurriedly noted down.

We again turned to our friendly Gujarati-speaking shopkeeper for help, who offered us two motorbikes being ridden by young lads who would deliver us to this pick-up point. This was such a generous act of kindness offered by complete strangers, who said it was just their way of showing appreciation for the all the hard work being undertaken by our agencies in the cyclone-hit provinces.

We thanked them profusely and set off on the two bikes, riding through pitch-dark rocky roads until we arrived at a riverbank with a bridge washed away in the cyclone. We soon discovered that the enterprising locals had constructed a makeshift ferry, which was the only means for the motorbikes and us to get across the river. We somehow managed this tricky manoeuvre, one bike at a time – my nervousness in sharp contrast with the attitude of those riders, who clearly saw this as just another adventurous mission in their young lives. The ferryman asking them to switch off the headlights during the crossing to avoid attracting the attention of any sleeping crocodiles did little to calm those nerves! Anyway, I did survive to tell the tale.

We arrived at our designated pick-up spot and were collected in time for me to join the Madagascar President's tour of the cyclone-hit villages the following day. However, as it turned out, the crocodile-infested river crossing was not the only brush with death on that mission. Later, I joined the President of the local Ismaili Council on his small, single-engine propeller plane to deliver supplies to another remote part of the island. As we prepared to land, I began searching for a runway amid an overgrown patch of grass where the plane seemed to be headed towards. Turns out, that is exactly where we were to land – on a makeshift runaway cleared of some of the grass. The pilot was clearly used to these unusual landings, taking his time bursting through clouds to give his plane a little wash before finally landing – the lurches up and down adding to the trepidation of his passengers.

All these eventful journeys helped us meet our targets and, in fact, we also undertook an assessment of two or three schools that could benefit from some rehabilitation support in the longer term. The enduring legacy of this mission was the symbolism of Christian and Muslim agencies working together to deliver humanitarian assistance to people in desperate need – highlighting the human bonds that unite us all, beyond all religious divides.

Destruction

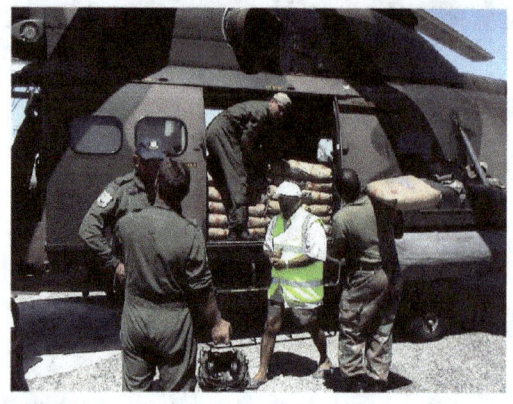

Volunteers briefing and transportation of food aid

Access to villages and distribution of food aid

Before and after rehabilitation of a school in partnership

Community participation leading to faces of hope.

Conclusion

Thus, we come towards the end of my journey through 40 years in the field of humanitarian work which, by the grace and abundance of God, has been both fulfilling and nourishing in equal measure. The narrative deliberately does not follow a chronological path, but instead a more geographical one. This is to highlight the common thread of the very different set of challenges posed by the terrain and indeed the political landscape of each milieu.

It has been a journey underpinned by spirituality that took in myriad modes of transport along the way – some fairly conventional, others quite bizarre and many within the realms of the absurd. A short flight from Khujand to Dushanbe in a 24-seater small twin-engine plane during my first visit to Tajikistan in 1995 ahead of His Highness' scheduled visit to the country is most certainly at the top of the absurd flights list. This was an aircraft packed with locals accustomed to commuting back and forth with their large brown gunny sacks of potatoes, onions and other farm produce.

As my colleague Zauhar and I boarded this rather unusual plane, which is perhaps best described as an air-taxi, it was soon apparent that we were in the minority as one of the few passengers keen to take a seat and fasten our seatbelts. Most of my co-passengers had a rather blasé approach to flying even as the pilot, or the gentleman in the driving seat for there was no pilot's uniform distinguishing him from the crowd, switched on the engine and made an announcement. His Russian pronouncements, a language alien to me at the time, resulted in many of my co-passengers standing up and placing their heavy hessian sacks on the seats instead. I soon gathered that they had been instructed by the pilot that their sacks should not be blocking the aisles. To my bemusement, they took this as a directive to stand through the duration of the flight with their farm produce placed on the seat instead. I need not elaborate on the sense of sheer relief that washed over me as soon as this air-taxi hit the tarmac in Dushanbe around 45 minutes later.

However, little did I know at the time that this reckless journey was just a precursor to some of the more treacherous travails that lay ahead. There was the trudging through snowcapped mountain passes, avalanches and mudslides, crossing crocodile infested and flooded rivers, dodging bullets in the crossfire of warring factions and ducking from missiles flying about. I can't help but feel extremely blessed that I survived to tell the tale and at least made every effort possible to try and live up to the name Farid (the unique one) that was bestowed upon me by His Highness the Aga Khan's grandfather Sir Sultan Mohamed Shah.

As for the sheer diversity of the modes of transport involved, I feel like I have covered just about all – from the more primitive donkey and horse ride up death-defying mountain tracks to the more routine single- and twin-engine UN planes. There were some rather dodgy helicopters, often flown by vodka-infused Russian pilots, as well as the military and cargo planes not especially designed to ferry civilians around and a snowbound UN helicopter in the middle of a flat plain in Afghan Badakshan. On the road, there were many bumpy rides on speeding motorcycles and quad bikes, sturdy 4X4 field vehicles and fully armoured and bullet-proof beasts. And inflatable dinghies and makeshift floats carrying essential supplies across choppy waters was par for the course.

The moments of having a Boeing B52 Bomber circle overhead while on the road or making assessments through a leaking old tunnel or braving through sandstorms and locust infestations in Afghanistan, what propelled me on was always our organisation's guiding motto: whatever it takes, aid must be delivered into the hands of the beneficiaries in a manner that preserves their dignity.

I embodied this mission, body and mind, in every natural disaster response and conflict or post-conflict zone I was deputed to. I can't say that having that unique vantage point to some of the worst human suffering did not take its toll. It is only to be expected that sleeping with the sound of bullets and missiles as an accepted night-time backdrop or the sight of a baby's stray shoe in a recently bombed town would result in some PTSD. It was after I was back in London after one of my many tours of a warzone that a psychiatrist pinpointed that my troubled sleep and anxiety attacks were the direct result of prolonged periods of being at the forefront of such stark human trauma.

However, I very consciously try and hold on to the many joys that over-rode the trauma – watching children's eyes light up with that Eureka! moment as a basic law of physics unfolds before their eyes or seeing smiles return to the faces of bereft families who find themselves with some shelter in the aftermath of a devastating natural disaster. In the toughest of scenarios, it is the quest of this tiny glimmer of hope that has kept me motivated throughout my decades in the field.

In my humble view, there can be no greater calling in life than to strive towards that hope which shines through from the depths of despair.

Epilogue

When I was offered the chance to connect with Farid to explore the contours of this memoir, I knew very little of the man behind these stories. Over the course of 12 months, multiple conversations ensued – some over cups of tea at his London home with his lovely wife D'jemilla and others of a more virtual nature on screen.

In hindsight, at the close of this enriching project, I can proudly say that it has been a real privilege to be taken deep into the warzones and behind the scenes of the familiar headlines of some of mankind's worst natural disasters. To say that Farid has led a fascinating life would be an understatement. He has stood witness to some of the biggest upheavals in recent history, be it the smashing of the Bamiyan Buddhas in Afghanistan or the aftermath of the Boxing Day Tsunami. There have also been several close shaves with death, more than an average individual's share to say the least.

However, what stood out with each chapter that he narrated was his stoicism through it all. I often had to probe extensively to be able to grasp the full extent of the danger that lurked behind his many humanitarian aid missions. He often recounted some of the most shocking and brave expeditions with a nonchalance that is clearly the outcome of being up close with danger far too many times to be able to dwell on the enormity of it all for many of us far removed from those first-hand experiences.

The pre-eminent emotion that best defines Farid's retelling of his humanitarian assignments is a profound sense of duty, shared in equal measure by D'jemilla. Asked how she coped with her husband's radio silences knowing he was somewhere deep into a warzone, especially during the days pre-dating mobile phone connectivity, D'jemilla responded with the same equanimity as her husband – 'I knew he was doing his duty'.

It is no wonder that this shared sense of duty and commitment to a higher cause created a partnership that resulted in such long-lasting impact on the ground. While many of the troubled zones Farid worked in continue to struggle to this day, the foundations of the AKDN that he laid in those hamlets, villages, towns and cities will undoubtedly stand the test of time.

I have tried to do complete justice to his incredibly inspiring life journey and hope that it can serve to motivate others to step into the field of humanitarian assistance. In his own words, it is not just a job but a true calling, and an extremely satisfying life mission.

■ *Aditi Khanna is a London-based journalist and writer, with many years of experience as a Foreign Correspondent for Indian and South Asian publications.*

About AKDN

The Aga Khan Development Network (AKDN) is dedicated to improving the quality of life of those in need, mainly in Asia and Africa, irrespective of their origin, faith, or gender. Our multifaceted development approach aims to help communities and individuals become self-reliant.

Founder and Chairman

His Highness the Aga Khan, the founder and chairman of the Aga Khan Development Network (AKDN), is the 49th hereditary Imam (Spiritual Leader) of the Shia Imami Ismaili Muslims. For His Highness the Aga Khan, one manifestation of his hereditary responsibilities has been a deep engagement with development for more than 60 years.

> Development is sustainable only if the beneficiaries become, in a gradual manner, the masters of the process. This means that initiatives cannot be contemplated exclusively in terms of economics, but rather as an integrated programme that encompasses social and cultural dimensions as well. Education and skills training, health and public services, conservation of cultural heritage, infrastructure development, urban planning and

> rehabilitation, rural development, water and energy management, environmental control, and even policy and legislative development are among the various aspects that must be taken into account.
>
> His Highness The Aga Khan

AKDN Annual Highlights:

• Deliver 8 million outpatient visits through more than 700 health facilities

• Provide early childhood development to over 2.3 million preschool children

• Teach nearly 1 million students through 200 schools and 2 universities

• Provide safe water to over 770,000 people

• Generate 1.8 billion kWh of clean electricity

• Provide financial services to over 50 million people

• Train 40,000 community volunteers in disaster management & response

• Plant over 3.2 million trees

FOCUS Humanitarian Assistance

As an affiliate of AKDN, FOCUS collaborates closely with several of its agencies and programmes. FOCUS also works with a number of other like-minded institutions and donor partners. These include partner government and government agencies, NGOs, as well as corporations that share an interest in the effort to provide relief and support services during and following natural and man-made disasters.

FOCUS was founded in 1994 by the Ismaili Community under the guidance of His Highness Prince Karim Aga Khan. Currently, it operates in Central and South Asia, Europe and North America to support emergency relief, principally in the developing world. The organisation serves people in need by reducing their dependence on humanitarian aid and facilitating their transition to sustainable, self-reliant and long-term development.

Over nearly two decades, FOCUS has grown on a global level into a multifaceted organisation, providing relief and assistance following avalanches, landslides, mudflows, earthquakes, cyclones, hurricanes, floods and wildfires. FOCUS has also undertaken successful resettlement programmes for displaced families and extended relief and recovery support for communities living in vulnerable environments.

The mission is: to save lives, reduce suffering and create resilience in communities prone to man-made or natural disasters. The main purpose is encompassed in the FOCUS vision statement: to become a seamless world-class community-based emergency humanitarian assistance organisation capable of delivering an increasing number of effective programmes and projects that save and protect lives, alleviate suffering and deprivation, facilitate refugee resettlement and repatriation, and facilitate disaster risk reduction measures in communities prone to man-made or natural disasters. This is achieved through endeavours in disaster risk reduction, disaster response, refugee and internally displaced persons assistance and operational strengthening.

- Source: The AKDN; FOCUS

www.ingramcontent.com/pod-product-compliance
Lightning Source LLC
Chambersburg PA
CBHW052019070526
44584CB00016B/1824